JUDSON PRESS

PUBLISHERS SINCE 1824

D1110221

THE WORK OF THE GREETER

PAIGE LANIER CHARGOIS

JUDSON PRESS
PUBLISHERS SINCE 1824
VALLEY FORGE, PA

The Work of the Greeter

© 2009 by Judson Press, Valley Forge, PA 19482-0851
All rights reserved.

Bible quotations in this volume are from the following versions: Unless otherwise indicated, HOLY BIBLE: *New International Version,* copyright © 1973, 1978, 1984 by International Bible Society; used by permission of Zondervan Bible Publishers. *The Holy Bible,* King James Version (KJV). The New King James Version (NKJV), copyright © 1982 by Thomas Nelson, Inc. The *Holy Bible,* New Living Translation (NLT), copyright © 1996, 2004 by Tyndale Charitable Trust; used by permission of Tyndale House Publishers; all rights reserved. The New Revised Standard Version (NRSV) of the Bible, copyright © 1989 by the Division of Christian Education of the National Council of the Churches of Christ in the U.S.A.; used by permission.

Library of Congress Cataloging-in-Publication Data
Chargois, Paige Lanier, 1944-
The work of the greeter / Paige Lanier Chargois.—1st ed. p. cm.
Includes bibliographical references. ISBN 978-0-8170-1540-4 (pbk.: alk. paper) 1. Church greeters. 2. Hospitality—Religious aspects—Christianity. I. Title. BV705.C43 2009
264—dc22   2009014467

Printed in the U.S.A.
First Edition, 2009.

To my beloved mother,
Blanche Louise Barham Lanier

Mom left a legacy of hospitality to her family by having never turned away a stranger and having entertained invited guests from near and far. Her example clearly demonstrated that hospitality is not about what one has but about how one uses what one possesses—without apology—for the benefit of others. It's not about the silver or crystal you may put out or how elaborate the effort; rather, the richest experience of hospitality is about the effort of drawing the stranger into your midst and enabling him or her to feel a sense of commonality with you and what you are endeavoring. That seed was planted at the tender age of six when I saw her welcome the first international guests into our meager domain. In subsequent years, she refocused my emphasis on the quality of hospitality from what I have or didn't have to a spirit of welcoming the stranger into who we are.

Thanks, Mom.

CONTENTS

ACKNOWLEDGMENTS

Churches across the nation immediately responded to my inquiry concerning their greeters' organization. From small congregations to mega-churches, there was an eagerness to share what they have experienced in launching, training, and sustaining such a significant ministry. I particularly would like to express my gratitude to the following churches:

- Willow Creek Community Church, South Barrington, Illinois
- Lakewood Church, Houston, Texas
- The Potter's House, Dallas, Texas
- Saddleback Community Church, Lake Forest, California
- New Birth MBC, Lithonia, Georgia
- Trinity United Church of Christ, Chicago, Illinois

Those who bear the responsibility of directing the greeters at these churches were kind and generous in sharing what they have experienced as well as what they are enjoying in that ministry. Heartfelt thanks to churches in the Richmond, Virginia, area, including First Baptist Church, South Richmond, and to John Hart, who served many years as the head usher at St. James Episcopal Church, for his rich insights gleaned from years of leadership. This list is not exclusive because I am also grateful to the many parishioners whose comments about their church's greeter ministry were insightful from the receiver's perspective.

Personal experience and observations at a variety of churches have contributed to and seasoned my thinking about the ministry of greeting. Reflection on these efforts has lifted my horizons about where this ministry yet needs to go if it is to greet worshipers more meaningfully in all congregations. Some of you have invited help and greater training so that your greeter ministry could become more inviting, efficient, and exciting. It is my hope that you will find what you need in this book to accomplish those ends.

Cathy Cawley is the director of Shalom House retreat center in Montpelier, Virginia, where I have taken many church groups who to want to return because of the quality and depth of hospitality they experience while attempting to plan and do the work of the Master as well to grow in their faith. Cathy awakened in them and in this writer the profound importance of a quality of hospitality for those questing to serve the cause of Christ our Lord, whether extended over a weekend or the flash of a moment just before worship. Hence, the many experiences there and the sharing of her thoughts with me were a profound source of inspiration in the writing of this book. For that I am eternally grateful.

Hospitality is in the core of my being regardless of the venue: whether home, office, or sanctuary, biblical faith requires us to be hospitable to the stranger in our midst while not neglecting the person once that stranger has become a part of our home or membership. May God's grace—the foundation of hospitality—continue to emanate through us as goodness and kindness, and may we find great joy in manifesting that grace to one and to all who seek to worship and to become, we hope, part of a kind, good, and loving Christian community.

INTRODUCTION

Church is changing. The anointing is flowing from the pulpit to the parking lot and from the chancel to the curb. The concept of ministry is broadening beyond preaching, singing, evangelism, and missions. Parishioners' needs of the moment are being considered seriously. In the attempt to retain and gain members, churches are becoming not only socially warmer but ever more sensitive to the quality of welcome they extend. Congregations are choosing to become a bit less formal as they launch new greeter ministries and activate greeting moments even during worship services. What we previously understood as ushering is coming under greater consideration and is being raised to new levels—or broadened into new forms of greeting—that seek to engage all who enter to worship.

This book will fully embrace the work of the greeter from scriptural expectations to cultural and social changes that influence the dynamics of church greeting ministries. In chapter 1, the role of the greeter will be presented from the perspective of history and Scripture. This chapter also explores the character of hospitality. Focus on the individual servant is examined in chapter 2, "The Character of the Greeter." Suggested qualifications of greeters will be offered.

In chapter 3, the character of your church is the topic. Although churches within the same denomination may have many similarities, their differences can be pronounced because of differences in size, location, ethnicity, religious, and cultural traditions. This chapter will help you evaluate your church context and discern how you will be able to fit into it a viable greeters' ministry.

No matter how small a congregation might be, your members and visitors deserve a level of excellence that reflects your love for God. No matter what distinguishes you as a congregation within your community, no demographic or economic description should diminish or usurp your ability to provide warmth and care to all who enter in. Whether two, or twenty, or two hundred folk are on your greeters' roster, there is no lessening of expectation within the mind, heart, or spirit of those who enter to worship relative to how they should be greeted.

Over the years, ushering has served a practical function to get people in place before "the real deal" of preaching, singing, and offerings took place. Ushers coordinated an easy, reverent, intermittent flow of worshipers during those times. Some aspects of ushering have already begun to morph into a more spiritual dimension—called greeting—because it is now being seen as the great ground of preparation for the spirit of those coming into worship. While ushers have traditionally provided bulletins as they escorted or directed parishioners to their seats, greeters help to set a tone of friendliness and acceptance from the parking lot or narthex to the sanctuary door. In my experience, it seems that how people are greeted and what they see in the greeting space does affect, positively or negatively, their immediate readiness to worship. Far more than a simple bulletin, a handshake or smile is essential to prepare God's people for a divine encounter.

This book will provide every possible detail to assist you in the organization of the work of greeters. Chapter 4 will cover launching a new greeters' ministry to sustaining it or possibly revamping what you have already developed. You will then be presented with suggestions, ideas, and concrete, practical tasks before and after the service (chap. 5), as well as looking at the greeters' ministry or tasks in the worship service (chap. 6).

No redemptive work or a Christian's servant role is without some challenges. Chapter 7 will help you look with clear eyes at what those challenges might be within your church. It will offer ways you might seek to meet some of the common difficulties and surmount some of the anticipated obstacles as you tackle common challenges in the work.

My aim is to prepare you practically for your greeters' ministry and to help prepare you spiritually as a servant of the Most High. Spiritual growth is essential for your well-being and for the success of your service to the congregation. We will seek to nurture that growth in chapter 8, "Spiritual Development of the Greeter." This, I believe, is a significant value in this book, and potentially this chapter can contribute much to you as a believer while you serve in the capacity of greeter.

In conclusion, what you will discover is that greeters in small churches have the privilege of helping worshipers have a big-church feeling of warmth and generosity of spirit. Greeters in big churches have the privilege of helping worshipers have a personal experience so that they will not be overwhelmed by the expanse of a cathedral-sized building. At either end of that spectrum, greeters are on hand to personalize and deepen the experience of each worshiper.

Since major new trends are not just on the horizon but are already present, active, and fully functioning within many congregations across the nation, this book will offer you more than just training. It will offer you the richness of spiritual hospitality that is rooted in the Bible, and not just culture: dimensions of care that are integral to our Christian faith. I welcome you to the ministry of greeting, knowing that you will help prepare arriving people for worship and turn strangers into family.

CHAPTER 1

The Role of the Greeter

Stepping into your role as a greeter, you may think that the ministry of greeting is as new as the emergence of it at your church or a neighboring church. You may think it's a new task to involve more people in the ministry of the church, but you may not be aware that it is deeply rooted in the Judeo-Christian faith. God instructed the Israelites to heed the needs of the stranger in their midst: "When an alien lives with you in your land, do not mistreat him. The alien living with you must be treated as one of your native-born. Love him as yourself, for you were aliens in Egypt. I am the LORD your God" (Leviticus 19:33-34). In *The Jews in Their Land*, David Ben-Gurion connects hospitality with the morality of the Israelites and each believer:

> The moral concept was certainly not the discovery or exclusive possession of the prophets or of the Jewish people as a whole. It belongs to [humanity]. But what particularizes it is the elevation of morality to the level of the supreme and omnipotent power that upholds and directs human life on all levels—the status of the individual, the relationship between [people] and [their] neighbor[s], the behavior of society as a whole, the relationship

between nation and nation, and, finally, the relationship between [an individual] and his [or her] God.[1]

With church life becoming less formal and more attention being given to relationships within churches, a new day has dawned for the greeter. New trends are emerging as ministers move beyond looking for smiling faces to testing volunteers for their giftedness in the ministry of hospitality. A task that previously was viewed as requiring minimal skill and ability—and even less spiritual orientation or Christian maturity—is now being viewed through the prism of ministry and spiritual gifts.

Your role has emerged as well out of an expansion of ushering. Previously, a smile, a bulletin, and an occasional handshake were thought to be sufficient as ushers stood in the doorways of the sanctuary awaiting the arrival of worshipers. As congregations grew into mega-churches, the onus was upon them to be or become personal and intimate to prevent people from getting lost in the attending crowds. Such crowds overwhelm the capabilities of ushers, and for a growing number of congregations, greeters are being added to their outreach ministries. Perhaps another consideration is that people will and do travel miles to go to the church of their choice rather than the church in proximity. This makes people more of a stranger then they would be in a neighborhood or community church a few blocks away from home.

Front Line, First Impressions

Greeters are "first impression" people. You are the front line for your pastor and your congregation. In the mind of the visitor, you are the official representative of your church, an ambassador, if you will. How you present yourself is how newcomers will imagine your congregation to be. Although it may seem that people are merely streaming in to make it to their chosen seat or pew before worship begins, be well aware that they are taking in how they are being approached, handled, directed, and greeted while they are on their way. You are not an usher preparing to march to the tunes of the choir, but, more importantly, <u>you are to be in tune with the needs of people arriving for wor</u>ship.

Greeting is not just a smile or a few nice words. It is welcoming folk into the space where they can be affirmed as children of God and be encouraged in their journey of faith. Greeting in the Christian church is entering the space of the total person, not stopping at the fringe with a handshake. Scriptures suggest and we are well aware that people's lives are changed by the grace they experience via the hospitable manners of a caring host. My hope is that more of that grace will be offered from the church through your ministry of greeting. Exude the Christian warmth that is made possible by the grace that God has given you that day!

The Grace to Care

More practically, the grace to care is an orientation toward a person and a focus upon his, her, or their immediate needs, if any—from handling a wet umbrella to helping with a baby to saying "Welcome!" or responding with appropriate information to worshipers' inquiries as they enter the church. A step toward the person with an extended hand orients you toward them, opens the encounter, and sets up your help in preparing them to enter the sanctuary for worship. At first glance, you will see whether the person is walking alone, has children in tow or a babe in arms, has a wet umbrella, seems confused or displaced, or demonstrates some difficulty walking. As a greeter, you should be able to read these fairly obvious needs immediately and offer the appropriate help. The response will open the conversation to define the help needed or reassure the greeter that he or she is all right. With that assured response, you have fulfilled your role as a greeter.

The grace to care for people emotionally will encourage you to read the kind of emotion being expressed by or reflected in their faces. Then it is incumbent upon you to respond in ways that either share in those emotions or address them as needed:

> when you see a smiling face—smile back!
> when you see a frowning or troubled face—
> show concern!
> when you see a puzzled or inquiring face—inquire
> or provide information!
> when you see a harried or frustrated face—offer
> consoling words!
> when you see a face in pain—offer a chair or inquire
> about the malady!

Such responses indicate that you have the grace sufficient to care without any sense of people needing to earn your help because of who they are, how they present themselves, or for any outward quality they may or may not possess. None of these are good starting points for worship. Why let them wade through half of the service before warming up to God and opening up to what the Holy Spirit wants to do in their lives? You—the greeter—can transform their outer countenance and their inner condition just by greeting them with grace—the grace to care.

The Character of Hospitality

The character of hospitality is not to be found in a Martha Stewart television program or at a luxurious hotel at which you are a paying guest. The essence and quality of hospitality that we should be willing to shower upon others is biblically based and an integral part of the faith to which all of Scripture calls every believer. In the Old Testament, hospitality is integrated into biblical law, while in the New Testament it becomes a natural expression of our love for God—a confession that must be demonstrated in the lives of others.

A fundamental biblical text, with which we are all familiar, is the telling of the foot washing at the Last Supper. This text has a far broader perspective than our focus in this book. It reaches to the core of every believer, no matter the task in the church. You may feel free to read the entire section found in John 13:1-17; however, it is the third sentence that recently captured my attention even after having read this text numerous times over the years: "It was just before the Passover Feast. Jesus knew that the time had come for him to leave this world and go to the Father. Having loved his own who were in the world, *he now showed them the full extent of his love*" (John 13:1, emphasis added).

Reflect on that last sentence for a moment. All these years we have been taught that the cross is the supreme demonstration of

Jesus' love for us. And that conclusion is biblically and theologically sound. John 3:16 reveals that "God so loved the world that he gave his one and only Son," which expresses the sacrifice of Jesus on the cross. We see another layer of that sacrifice when we read of Jesus in Gethsemane, where everything within him militated against his going to the cross all the way up to his, "Nevertheless!" The cross satisfied God the Father's demonstration of love to us and God the Son's love for his Father.

However, it is in John 13—his disrobing, wrapping a towel around his waist, picking up a basin with some water to wash the disciples' feet—that Jesus showed yet another layer of love and sacrifice. Healing blinded eyes, feeding hungry thousands, cleaning out the temple, and casting out demons were demonstrations of his power. But the washing of dirty feet revealed no miraculous power; instead, by this deed Jesus demonstrated the quality and depth of his love.

In that culture, the lowest of the lowliest servants had the task of washing feet, which could get filthy by walking through garbage and animal droppings. So, when visitors arrived, it was the responsibility of the host to provide for a cleansing of the feet. However, the host never performed that task. It was too demeaning!

This larger text has often been summarily tagged as the model for Christian servanthood. And that it is. But it's far more. Jesus clearly demonstrates that in the face of others' needs, we must have the capability to diminish ourselves momentarily in allowing for the personal provision and care of others. Such a gesture demands an inner capacity and quality of love that far exceeds mere servanthood and humility. It demands of every believer and servant of God a depth of spirit and flexibility of personhood that supersedes even Paul's experience: "I know how to be abased, and I know how to abound" (Philippians 4:12 NKJV). It's not about being treated poorly but of having the will— motivated by love—to take oneself to the lowest possible human rank for the well-being of another human soul. What other text better mirrors for us the best way to fulfill our roles in the church regardless of the task at hand?

The biblical epistles address some aspects of hospitality from a celebrative rather than an instructive perspective. Still, as Paul pens his many letters to nascent churches, the expectation of hospitality is consistent. In Philippians 2:29, believers are told to "welcome him in the Lord with great joy," and in Romans 12:13, Paul tells believers to "share with God's people who are in need. Practice hospitality." In 1 Peter 4:9, the directive is to "offer hospitality to one another without grumbling." Though they may not know these Bible verses, strangers or guests should be able to expect these things when they enter into your church.

It was important for Paul to infuse the grace of the Lord into the ways Christians greeted one another. At the beginning of nearly all of his letters, Paul declared "grace and peace to you" (Romans 1:7; 1 Corinthians 1:3; 2 Corinthians 1:2; Galatians 1:3; Ephesians 1:2; Philippians 1:2; Colossians 1:2; 1 Thessalonians 1:1; 2 Thessalonians 1:2; 1 Timothy 1:2; 2 Timothy 1:2; Titus 1:4; Philemon 3). The church at Colosse was addressed as "the holy and faithful," and Paul offered "grace and peace to you from God our Father." Paul implored Titus to "greet those who love us in the faith." That opening moment was to be special, but more than that it was to open up the greater possibility of encountering God as one prepared to enter worship. Occasionally Paul would name several individuals to whom he was sending special greetings or from whom special greetings were being sent (2 Timothy 4:19-21). In his closing instructions and benedictions, believers were encouraged to "greet…one another" (Romans 16; 1 Corinthians 16; Philippians 4:21-22; Colossians 4:10-18; 2 Timothy 4:19-21; Titus 3:15; Philemon 23-24). In three letters, he told believers to "greet one another with a holy kiss" (1 Corinthians 16:20; 2 Corinthians 13:12; 1 Thessalonians 5:26).

For a sublime example of hospitality, consider the church that met in the home of Philemon, to which Paul wrote:

> I always thank my God when I pray for you, Philemon, because I keep hearing about your faith in the Lord Jesus and your love for all of God's people. And I am praying that you will put into action the generosity that comes from your faith as you understand and experience all the good things we have in Christ. Your love has given me much joy and comfort, my brother, for your kindness has often refreshed the hearts of God's people. (Philemon 4-7 NLT)

Few New Testament passages could be as foundational as that one to a greeters' ministry—making people feel welcome in the house of the Lord with some level of lavishness rather than with a limited perspective of a salutation. How beautifully Paul alluded to acts of generosity that emanate from our faith "as [we] understand and experience all the good things we have in Christ." The list of good things that we experience in Christ Jesus is potentially inexhaustible. Yet any and all of these good things surely undergird our desire for and ability to carry out the ministry of greeting. We have two thousand years of evidence that such good things not only bring "much joy and comfort" to people, but as well, such kindness is often refreshing to "the hearts of God's people."

The Art of Diplomacy

Your role as a greeter also is rooted in diplomacy, which the Merriam-Webster dictionary defines as "the art and practice of conducting negotiations between nations" and "skill in handling affairs without arousing hostility" (tact). Diplomats of any country are steeped in the language and culture of the country they represent but also of the country in which they will serve. At embassies and consulates around the world, they function on two levels as they seek to befriend the foreigner and resolve the immediate official problems of guests to that country. In the context of the church, Richard N. Longenecker perhaps puts it best: "whether the problem is material or spiritual, love requires of us immediate and unquestioning help."[2] As a front-line, first-impressions person, the greeter is visitor-oriented and yet supportive of members as they, too, arrive for worship. And, although the ministry of the greeters seems new, it is well established in our faith as both a moral and spiritual expectation. Saddleback Church declares that "a softened heart is an open heart, and greeters serve God by helping…people receive His Word."[3] As an ambassador, show that openness of heart to those you greet. It takes grace to do so!

In the House of God

Would you believe that the first church was a tent? It was called the tabernacle, and it confirmed the presence of God in the midst of his people. In Exodus 25:8, God said, "And let them make me a sanctuary, that I may dwell among them." Remembering the tabernacle will do much to awaken you to the quality of hospitality you are meant to fulfill as a greeter.

Exodus 25, 26–27, 31, and 35–39 are filled with specific instructions about how God wanted the tabernacle built and what he wanted in it, even to the point of specifying the kind of wood and how many rings were to be made for the ark of the covenant, in which God's law was stored. This might suggest to us that the act of greeting folk and welcoming worshipers into God's space is to be—or to become—sensitive to detail. That will also encourage us to have a sense of orderliness: about ourselves, our greeters, our ushers, the sanctuary, the chairs and pews. Is everything in order? Have you managed the necessary details?

Those passages also tell us that the Israelites gave generously to the work of building the tabernacle by contributing precious metals or specific skills, such as weaving or carpentry. From this we might conclude that we, too, can give our best efforts to the task to which we are called.

At the dedication of the tabernacle, "the cloud covered the tent of meeting, and the glory of the LORD filled the tabernacle"

(Exodus 40:34 NRSV). Though "even heaven and the highest heaven cannot contain" God (1 Kings 8:27 NRSV), this physical structure symbolized the presence of God with the Israelites and functioned as the place where Israel offered sacrifices and, above all, worshiped the Lord. The Scriptures emphasize God's house as a "house of prayer for all nations" (e.g., Isaiah 56:7), and in your work as a greeter, you can help worshipers to enter God's house with calm, prayerful minds and hearts.

Be Mindful of the Doors

As a greeter, you will need to be mindful of the doors of the church, practically and spiritually, sometimes asking yourself whether to stand inside, or outside, or at the doors of the church. Practically your decisions might depend upon the weather and/or how the mass of people flow through those doors. And those decisions can be easily made and adapted. However, as a greeter you might also want to sensitize yourself to the spiritual importance of and symbolic nature of doors in Scripture. The first doors mentioned are the doors of the ark (Genesis 6:16), and the last mention is in Revelation 4:1: "there before me was a door standing open in heaven." And in between the two, Jesus declares, "I tell you the truth, I am the gate for the sheep. All who ever came before me were thieves and robbers, but the sheep did not listen to them. I am the gate; whoever enters through me will be saved. He will come in and go out, and find pasture. The thief comes only to steal and kill and destroy; I have come that they may have life, and have it to the full" (John 10:7-10).

It would serve greeters well to be sensitized to these major openings to human salvation and to God's domain. The first doors mentioned suggest a sense of safety when Noah, his family, and the animals entered the doors of the ark. The last doors are the ones through which believers pass into their ultimate reward: to live with God throughout eternity. However, Jesus' words are suggestive of nurture as well as salvation. Consequently, the doors of your church need to be well managed relative to "the sheep" who are coming "in and out" to be nourished by the Word.

As a greeter, be mindful that people entering into worship are not just coming through your doors. They are coming out of something they have left behind just to be able to worship God at your church. For some, it is no small thing out of which they emerge as they make their way into worship. For others, what they have left behind might be trivial to someone else but significant to them. Far more important than the actual doors is the fact that you must remember your function as a door allowing people to enter and worship. Understanding that will allow you to be more sensitive in your role as greeter.

Abraham and Sarah, the first worshipers of the God to whom we trace our faith, were nomads! Homeless people! Yet they were moving according to a promise and toward a horizon that God had created for their future. Your duty as a greeter, should you choose to accept it, is to first of all greet those who may not be technically homeless but have left their homes—their places of dwelling. As they enter your doorways, they are now moving toward the horizon of hope, even toward a promise they have heard from God about their lives.

In your role as a greeter, be aware that you are helping to shape the community of faith within the expectation of the gospel and in the practices of the church from its beginning. Luke 7:36-50 tells of the experience of Jesus as he visits a Pharisee who had invited him for a meal. Jesus strongly contrasts the unknown woman who lavished appropriate hospitality upon him with the host and others who only complained of the attention Jesus was receiving. Jesus framed the matter as one of appropriate hospitality but also within the context of gratitude. Alluding to God's grace, Jesus compared and contrasted the quality of hospitality to the amount of grace each one has experienced in their relationship with God. The quality of hospitality that you have received from God, and the gratitude you offer in return, is reflected in the quality of hospitality you show to those who enter the doors of God's house.

Body Language: Theirs and Yours

So, then, how do we meet people? How do we greet them? How do we welcome them into the house of the Lord? A prepared heart and spirit are essential. The mind, appropriate body language, and order will follow.

No matter the scowl that may be on their faces, or the angry words you happen to overhear, or the rushed, impatient demeanor you plainly see, the reality is that people have left home to move towards a more glorious horizon within God's promises to them of hope for their lives. As John the Baptist did for Jesus, "make straight [their] way" (John 1:23). Remove any obstacle—physical, verbal, or attitudinal—that might hinder their worship.

Have you ever considered all that most people have to work through to get to the church door?

> Should I get up or not?
> Should I shower? bathe? neither?
> Should I eat or have a cup of coffee or nothing?
> Do I leave the dishes for later?
> Should I dress up or dress down?
> Is this dress acceptable? shirt? pants? clean? ironed?
> Do I have enough gas?
> What does my hair look like?

Now, if they have to go through all of that and more—not even considering what they might go through during their drive to the church or in the church parking lot—be thankful that they made it across the church threshold to worship the Lord. An attitude of thanksgiving and grace is sufficient to greet them. Every soul entering is a victory for Jesus and a clear defeat for his enemy because those entering have overcome what could have been obstacles preventing them from coming to worship the Lord. As greeters, we ease the journey of life, not just the entryway into the sanctuary.

Practical Preparations
Such considerations should help you to prepare the narthex, where you would usually greet worshipers. Many young mothers have bundles of childcare items in hand or more than one child they are trying to handle—perhaps even a baby their in

arms. Some elderly worshipers may have difficulty walking or managing the door, or they have parcels with which help might be needed. As you enter their space—the immediate space around them—your discernment should lead you to offer practical help that is needed at that time.

This is an important part of training, and a sufficient amount of greeters should be on duty so that the greeting area is not left unattended when one or perhaps several greeters at a time might be needed to offer such help. Let this be a part of your planning, including alerting another greeter that help is needed to get a worshiper to a particular place.

Emotional and Spiritual Preparation of the Greeter
I like the definition of "emotion" that Wikipedia offers:

> An **emotion** is a mental and physiological state associated with a wide variety of feelings, thoughts, and behaviors. It is a prime determinant of the sense of subjective well-being and appears to play a central role in many human activities.

Greeting is surely one activity in which emotions can and do factor into our behavior. As a greeter, you are encouraged to be prepared emotionally by exhibiting the "fruit of the Spirit": love, joy, peace, patience, gentleness, goodness, meekness, self-control, and faith (Galatians 5:22-23). Your growth as a Christian, as well as a greeter, can often be measured by the degree that these qualities inform your personal life and ministry.

Though this subject will be covered more deeply in chapter 8, let me touch on it here in this context. You are encouraged to prepare yourself spiritually so that you might be discerning of people's needs and possess the spiritual strength to address those needs rather than ignore them in an effort to just shake hands with all who are entering the church. When people cross that threshold, nothing but your smile, your warmth, your welcoming hand, your Christian love, and the Spirit of the living Christ should greet them.

Selflessness is the order of the day: the needs of self are relegated to a much lower priority than the needs of others. What you have had to overcome in order to get to church is not important once you mount your post. By now, we hope, you have, with your team, conquered all of the negatives you encountered and that might have infected your disposition on your way to serve the people of the Lord. You confess what is troubling or hindering you, offer it to the Lord in prayer as a sacrifice (something you want to relinquish to him and be free of), and then invite the Holy Spirit to give you that sustaining and conquering power in your preparation to serve God's people. As you are transformed by God's grace, you will have sufficient grace to give to others.

Transform people's moment of arrival, and you will open their souls to worshiping the Lord in a profound way. The way they are greeted will influence how and/or how soon they will be open to worship the Lord in the service. Open your heart, free your spirit, and empty your mind of all hindering thoughts to being on duty to greet God's people and those who are potential candidates for God's kingdom. More than mere words, warmth is needed to help them know they are truly welcomed into the house of the Lord!

CHAPTER 2

The Character of the Greeter

Presidents, governors, mayors, senators, representatives, some clergy, and many other public personalities have all been in the news over the recent past not as much for lack of ability as for weakness of character. From lies to bribery to misrepresentation of facts, one after another has fallen into a painful display of a lack of good, strong character. They have done things we never expected, and we are still shocked that some of them could do such things. Leaders at whatever level are not immune to bad character traits or free from character flaws. They have given in to their weaknesses rather than living in their strengths and choosing to allow their lives to be characterized not just by the good that they do but more by the quality of character they present to the world every day.

It begs the question, "What is character?" I like the definition in Webster's dictionary best, that character is "the aggregate of distinctive qualities," qualities that stand out and have a positive net effect upon others. These would be qualities that we admire in others and that others admire in us—the best of who we can be to one another and in our faith relationship with Jesus Christ. The list of these aspects of our character or character traits seems almost endless and overwhelming. However, once we reflect upon them, these traits are natural and normal to us in our everyday lives, but some of them need more definition in our lives and/or refining through our learning or experiences.

With a million and one things to contemplate, decide, and get done, few of us give much thought to character in our day-to-day experiences. Yet, to one degree or another, our character is reflected in everything we think, say, and do. It is DNA found in a person's behavior wherever he is and regardless of what she is doing. One's character can be qualified as poor, good, or excellent or perhaps any variation between those three qualities. How sad that when we are older we might give character some thought but it is not all that important to us in our younger years. Perhaps it should be. Perhaps it isn't because we don't know how to handle such qualities proactively: we wince when people might choose to criticize one of our character traits, and we glow when someone chooses to praise them. All too often we simply move on to the next item on our agenda for the moment without realizing that such an encounter serves to help shape our character—positively or negatively.

Surfing the Internet recently I found a listing of 247 character traits[1] that amazed me. I could identify with virtually every one of them—after I looked up a couple of the words. I didn't know we had so many traits; I could have named a few, but not that many. Every single human behavior reveals a character trait that is present and currently operating or strong in a person's life. That being the case, it might behoove us to take a closer look at these possibilities particularly within the framework of being a greeter at our church. That service catapults you, like it or not, into a leadership role that represents both who and what your church is to those walking through your doors. Knowing that 247 traits were too many to talk about in this one chapter, I have selected 33 of those character traits that I believe are important to those serving in the role of greeter.

Conscientious	Polite	Dependable
Attentive	Responsive	Persistent
Hospitable	Considerate	Active
Compassionate	Useful	Confident
Cheerful	Dutiful	Positive
Happy	Cooperative	Peaceful
Enthusiastic	Tactful	Wise
Friendly	Sensitive	Mature
Helpful	Amiable	Affable
Respectful	Thoughtful	Jovial
Warmhearted	Faithful	Loving

I did not choose "religious" as one of the 33 because that is the last thing we need to be, and the list did not have "Christian" as an option, but there is a world of difference between the two. Our faith should not make us more religious; rather, it should make it less so. God's grace transcended "religion" in Jesus Christ and makes our faith not just something we do but who we are because we have been born again. You can commit to or be dedicated to any religion, but you can only be born into Christianity, which places relationship(s) above laws and rituals.

Why Is Character Important?

As a greeter, you are on the cutting edge of initiating and strengthening relationships for your church and within the kingdom of God. Each person walking through the doors of your church is already a child of God by creation and is potentially a sister or brother in the Lord if or when he or she accepts Jesus Christ as Savior. So relationships are vital in the church and to our faith, and many of those relationships may be launched at the doors of your church.

We struggle through life allowing our character to be formed without much intention on our part. It happens as we go along and face life. But is that the best way to become a person pleasing to God and a blessing to others? We can become far more intentional about who we are becoming as we represent not only our church but also ourselves, our families, the best of our friends, and our Lord.

People can see us with a glimpse or two and size up our character because each of these character traits becomes or serves as a window into who we are. Folk can and often do decide in that first encounter whether they want to get to know us better. They know within a nanosecond whether we have had a positive or negative impact upon them because character is not in a vacuum or hidden within. It is visible in how we relate to people we encounter and how we present ourselves to them.

It was the Greek philosopher Heraclitus who declared that "character *is* destiny!"[2] So wherever you might be going in your life, your character will either get you there or diminish your chances of success. If it is that important, then perhaps we should be more intentional about how it is developing in our lives. This is also why many people have said that success is not a destination but a journey. It requires much thought, determination, and being intentional about our growth and development to truly become the success we envision.

Becoming Effective

In Luke 8:1-3, Luke declares that Jesus had cured the three women named in the text "and many others." When the Lord taps people for service, he heals some of them of their maladies while others need deliverance from some hindering, even debilitating, behaviors. In *Certain Women Called by Christ: Biblical Realities for Today*,[3] I declare that we don't fully know what was meant by demons being cast out and could not name them if we tried with today's psychosocial understandings. But what we do know is that Jesus made folk who were demon-possessed effective instead of ineffective and cast off by much of society. So even today, our Lord is ready, willing, and able to make us more effective in whatever role and task to which he has called us.

He who has promised to give us a comforter, a paraclete, someone to walk with us and to reside within us to empower us to do the good he has called us to do, has clearly shown that our character is uppermost in his mind as he longs to shape us into an image that will glorify God.

You may not feel effective initially, but all that is required is that you be diligent in your efforts to grow, which will strengthen your ability to reach the level of effectiveness you desire. That's why being *conscientious* is so important. You cannot be conscientious without being *attentive*—discerning what's missing and endeavoring to supply what should be supplied. This would apply not only to your surroundings while greeting but also to your attire and your attitude. Being conscientious and attentive is to carefully allow your mind to consider every possible detail and your eyes to insure that such details are in place and are correct.

You are not alone in this because Jesus declared, "But when he, the Spirit of truth, comes, he will guide you into all truth" (John 16:13). These realities about which you are trying to be conscientious are not all up to you; part of the work of the Holy Spirit is to remind you and to draw your attention to such details, thereby enabling you to do your best, look your best, and be your best as unto the Master. There is no pressure on you as a believer or as a greeter; God is ready, willing, and able to raise you to new levels of being conscientious and attentive.

Your part is to "watch and pray so that you will not fall into temptation. The Spirit is willing but the body [flesh] is weak" (Matthew 26:41). This necessitates regular times of Bible study, private devotions, and prayer. These become your avenues for growth and moving into new levels of being effective.

Being Hospitable

Would you believe that being *hospitable* is a character trait? How you care for the stranger or visitor in your midst, as well as how you provide for those most familiar, is a character trait. This is one reason Jesus castigated the pharisaic host who was so inhospitable (not having supplied water for footwashing) and yet complained when someone outside of his household washed

Jesus' feet. The host was lacking not in skill as much as he was lacking in character. Skills can easily be developed; the problem is that they are not sufficiently employed without the strength of character to support them. Skills in greeting are not sufficient. Churches need greeters with the strength of character that is foundational to the ability to learn and harness the skills that have been taught.

A few other traits that factor into being hospitable include being *compassionate*—thinking more about the well-being of others than the comfort of one's self. Being *cheerful* is important as you seek to be a light in darkness, as Jesus called us to be in the Sermon on the Mount. You are a greeter to bring brightness, light, joy, and cheer to those entering your doors. You cannot make them happy, but if you are a *happy* person, that quality will most positively influence their lives as well.

Who can be hospitable without being *enthusiastic*? Hospitality goes out the window if it's not accompanied by some level of enthusiasm. Folk want to perceive that you are excited about their arrival and presence. Your *friendliness* will not be a cover for excitement and enthusiasm. The latter are deeper qualities than friendliness, which can potentially be a bit superficial in the role we are discussing.

Having lived in Germany for many years, I often heard Germans declare that Americans were friendly and outgoing when you first met them but then you would hit a stone wall in the relationship that you didn't expect. Germans, by contrast, were much more reserved in initial encounters, but once you penetrated that wall, you—in their words—had a friend for life.

At the door as greeters, measure your friendliness with degrees of being

helpful   responsive
respectful   considerate
warmhearted   useful
polite   compassionate

These additional character traits, when developed in great capacities, are strong building blocks in your ability to be friendly. The levels of care and concern you offer to arriving worshipers, demonstrating your unselfishness and that you are truly in your role to serve, will shine through your handshakes and smiles in a powerful way.

Being Dutiful

You know or are quickly learning your duties as a greeter, but the sense of being *dutiful*—of being committed to what you have signed up to do—will open up your ability to be *cooperative* with your leaders, your teammates, and those who are entering your church doors. When worshipers need your help with a child, with packages, with information, or with a chair to rest on, don't turn a deaf ear or a blind eye. Meet the need to the best of your ability or call on someone who can.

On occasion you may have an emergency; and your cooperation with levels of authority is paramount. You may need to call for additional help. Remaining faithful to meeting the need at the time is not only an expectation of your role as a greeter, your ability to do so also says much about your character.

Folk coming into your church would have an unspoken expectation of trust, of your being reliable and dependable as they enter the sanctuary to worship and possibly become members of your church. On occasion, you might need to check yourself with the question "Why am I here if not to be useful?"

A part of being dutiful is learning to be *tactful,* because everything that people bring into the house of the Lord is not appropriate. You will find that you might need to remind folk about their cell phones: to turn them off or not to talk on them within the narthex. Your ability to be tactful is part of your duty, but you can be *sensitive* and *amiable* while not seeking to offend but rather to intelligently and in a *thoughtful* way inform folk what is allowed and what is not allowed.

You're on the Team

Being *faithful* to your station as part of your team is important. Don't just accept your assignment, but be faithful to your assignment because the degree to which you are *dependable* is a reflection of the strength of your character. *Honesty* is the best policy because you will have to *persevere* sometimes in order to meet this and other obligations you have signed on to. If people cannot count on you, they don't need you! You want your teammates to be able to count on you because you have given them your commitment to serve. Being thankful that you have a wonderful opportunity to serve God's people, you want to remain an *active* and *confident* part of the team. Let the best of your character show through. Show up when scheduled, and remain on duty the appropriate amount of time. By doing this you serve as a *positive* role model for your greeter team. This will help to keep *peace* among the team because its members know they can count on one another.

Being *wise* is a character trait that factors in here because we are told that if we lack wisdom, "ask God, who gives generously to all without finding fault, and it will be given" (James 1:5). As we look to God in challenging moments or moments of decision, his Word declares that he gives us the wisdom we need both generously and without finding any fault in us. That certainly can usher in more *mature* decisions that we might be forced to make on the spot as we serve in our greeter role.

Personality Traits

A few of these so-called character traits seem to suggest types of personalities rather than qualities of character because some people seem naturally more *affable* or more *jovial* in their dispositions. However, upon closer scrutiny we will find that often they have worked at being more outgoing, or perhaps their kind of work, various situations, or growth have enabled them to be or become affable and jovial when they need to be. Be that as it may, these are admirable qualities that reveal a level of genuineness in moments of greeting.

Whatever your personality traits, they can be strengthened by growth and development of your character and enable you to be or become more sincere with those you encounter and with those whom you are privileged to serve. The more of yourself that you invest into these relationships, the more secure you help to make them. Though you may see your encounters with the people you greet or with other greeters as brief, do not discount the possibility that these will become important relationships over time. Though you are not there to make friends necessarily, you are there to be friendly and *loving*, which is one of the more powerful character traits.

We tend to think of our strong feelings as indications of strong character. Perhaps William Carleton, an Irish writer, says it best: "Strong feelings do not necessarily make a strong character. The strength of a man is to be measured by the power of the feelings he subdues not by the power of those which subdue him."[4]

More often our ability to control our strong feelings would be the greater indication of a quality of character. If you happen to become upset on duty or in meetings or with a teammate or leader of the greeters' ministry, you are encouraged to have the strength of character to put those feelings in check until an appropriate time is possible to deal with such matters.

This Job Requires Study

I've told many folk over the years: There is no problem in not knowing. The only problem is in not wanting to know. You will not make the progress you desire and need if you do not study your church's manual, know it completely, and follow its instructions, which should lead you to greater service and wonderful growth as a Christian and as a greeter. Don't just know your post. Know your church. Know your teammates. Know your leaders. Know your church family. Know your church activities, its ministries, its policies and operational procedures.

You grow in personal confidence as you commit to learning more about the ministry of greeting and more about your church. Don't accept the church handbook you have been given, and feel that you can walk into any situation on any Sunday morning and handle it. You need training. You need information. You need knowledge. You need experience. All of these require that you tap into your ability to become studious and enjoy learning about your new role as a greeter for the church and the people you love. This is how you become more confident in your role and are able to face your tasks with a level of preparedness and pride in a job well done.

Praise or Criticism

Get ready for both. We want to be lavished with praise and we hope that criticism is almost nonexistent, but that is not usually the case. Norman Vincent Peale shared a bit of his wisdom in the following statement: "The trouble with most of us is we would rather be ruined by praise than saved by criticism."[5]

With good training and regular practice or orientation, criticisms will be kept at a minimum and praise will be profuse. As an officer or a teammate, leading through encouragement is best for all. However, when criticism is needed, don't hold back, for issues do not fade away; they hang around to challenge you at times you least expect if they have not been sufficiently dealt with. Encourage openness and transparency as your team builds its relationships.

The character trait that I would add to the list is *courage*, which is your ability to do the right thing even as you might face difficulty. Let your conscience be your guide because just following the crowd in your thinking is truly a dead-end street. You may not often have the need to be courageous in this work as a greeter, but be prepared for when that time comes! Do not hesitate to confront difficult issues, but do so in a kind, generous, and loving way in the effort to rid yourself of the problem and not the person.

Your Core Values

As a team, begin to think together about the best values that can hold the team together. List those values, talk about them, narrow down the list, and finally agree on the irreducible minimum list of values that your greeters' ministry needs to function at its highest level. Never hesitate to remind people of their core values. Keep those values posted. Recite them. Print them in newsletters. Share them in bulletins. They should be the most meaningful values to you in your ability to fulfill your calling as a greeter.

Let the quality of your leaders reflect these core values. Elect people whose strength of character has qualities you can point to, laud, and share as examples of the kind of greeters desired throughout your team. Inspire your team to adhere to their shared values, and most of all to never neglect the value of prayer. When and where character might fail and even core values might prove insufficient, the power of prayer will rule the day and carry the moment. Prayer itself is our greatest asset—knowing the One who is greater than ourselves—and the strongest of our core values that will not allow us to give up on one another or fail at our task of greeting God's people. May God bless you in your diligent efforts to be effective and succeed!

CHAPTER 3

The Character of Your Church

How intimate *is* your knowledge of your church? You could easily describe a church, but how accurately could you describe *your* church? If you have been there fifty years, you might describe it from a historical perspective. If, however, you've been there five years, you would be more likely to describe it from a more spiritual perspective. If you've been there only five Sundays, most likely you would describe your church from the perspective of its personality, alluding to its warmth, friendliness, or kindness.

Every church possesses a quality of character that is unique and is often contextualized by its history, its ministries, its commitment to the Word in preaching and study opportunities, and/or its quality of care for those walking through its doors. The challenge is grasping the appropriate words that qualify and endeavor to describe what one sees as the true character of the church. Knowing this—verbalizing this—will provide focus and better comprehension of not only what you already have but also what the church yet needs specifically in regards to launching a greeters' ministry.

To find or identify the character of your church, consider the following: churches are often described by their spiritual temperature or by their level of friendliness. Some have been defined by the abundance of ministries and missions involvement or the lack thereof; yet others are described by their wealth or their poverty. Whether measured on a continuum from cold to hot or weighed on the scales of friendliness, you are encouraged to ask yourself, "Where is my church?" How would you characterize your congregation? How would you describe it to those outside of your church? What's unique about it? Is it easily definable? What strong qualities do you discern that are generally evident without having to think too long?

Well, I believe that to begin identifying the character of your church, you need to know the congregation and its worship and its ministries from these three perspectives: its depth, its breadth, and its reach beyond itself. Let's look at each perspective one at a time.

The Character of a Church

DEPTH What is the genesis point of your congregation? Did your church begin out of conflict or as a missions effort? Did it break from another congregation, or was it planted by those who knew that a church was needed in your community? Was it just the pastor and a few folk in someone's living room, or was it a clarion call to folk in one congregation to seed another? Read several writings of its history, and talk with at least five of the oldest members of the congregation to begin to ascertain what shaped this church from its beginnings. It has grown in several ways since then, but it probably has not moved far from the spirit in which it began.

BREADTH Over its history, what kind of person has been drawn to your congregation? There is much truth in the old adage that "birds of a feather flock together." You will find that folk who enjoy certain worship styles and certain styles of administration, degrees of openness to newcomers or not, the quality of Bible study/teaching, or style of music tend to comprise your congregation because within it they have found a certain spiritual comfort level. But they also need a certain cultural comfort level and must find a sense of fitting in to remain faithful to a particular congregation. Their level of activity and their success in functioning hinge greatly on their sense of fitting in and feeling a part of the church family.

OUTREACH Churches are sustained and to a great degree experience their significant growth by the degree of outreach in which they engage. The more church congregations cloister themselves and focus on their internal needs or the needs of those currently present, the more shrinkage inevitably occurs. The degree to which they reach beyond themselves in serious efforts of missions and various ministries to communities and to the world enlarges not only their perspectives but also their membership. Not only how congregations reach out but to whom would be critical considerations that either encourage greater involvement or minimize such involvement. The level of excellence and of success in these ministries is also a consideration in people's minds when they are viewing a church for prospective membership.

Depth, breadth, and outreach will help you to know the true character of your church and will provide significant insight into adding ministries such as a greeters' ministry to your offerings. So, as you have reflected on these three categories and the distinguishing characteristics of each, I hope you now have greater insight into the true character of your church. See if you can write that in a sentence or a phrase or a single word:

_____
sentence

_____
phrase

_____
word

WORD You have taken a mental snapshot of your church from the inside or from a long-standing or historical perspective. This perspective gives you a fairly solid idea of what and where your church is now. But put that camera into the hands of a visitor or two and a very different picture of your congregation might emerge. Can the two perspectives be reconciled? How similar are those snapshots, and how much of a contrast is revealed?

Whether through a survey of recent visitors, phone conversations with a few, or home visitations, endeavor to discern what visitors think of your worship, your warmth, and your witness to the community. Wherever you might land on the continuum in these three areas will significantly prepare you in launching your greeters' ministry. You will be better able to shape it in your training, orientation, and expectations seeking to meet the need of hospitality and influence other ministries of your congregation.

Launching a greeters' ministry will not correct every flaw you might find in your church. Neither will it assure you of hordes of new visitors. However, there is no doubt that a vital, vibrant, and valuable greeters' ministry will accomplish the following in varying degrees. It will:

- significantly affect visitor impression(s)
- help to transform visitors into members
- increase the perceived warmth of your congregation
- raise the level of excellence expected in your ministries
- provide perhaps the only opportunity for full families to serve together
- change the concept of hospitality from being food-centered to emphasizing fellowship, outreach, and care
- enable a significant cadre of members to move beyond themselves in new outreach
- help members to derive as much benefit as visitors
- instill pride and increase friendliness even among members
- heighten care about ministries
- deepen the overall quality of hospitality in your congregation.

A strong greeters' ministry is the quality of foundational ministry that lends support to all other ministries of the church. It spiritually connects people via human validation of worth and value by helping them to feel good about themselves and the quality of momentary care received from the church. Neither the deacons' ministry nor the missionaries' nor the ushers' ministry touches the number of folk that the greeters' ministry does. It could be considered to be the many-tentacled ministry with arms to reach into and connect with—that is, spiritually and socially influence—all other ministries of the church. The sustained quality of greeting opens up all parishioners to one another in various ways. Once their lives have been touched by the ministry of greeting, individuals carry that quality into other levels of office and organizational involvement to create a circle of warmth and influence in the church. Greater knowledge even about how to offer hospitality in other areas of the church will begin to emerge.

In *What Is Your Church's Personality?* Phillip Douglass declares that "your church's personality points to the most productive ministry path as you engage in your mission. Ministry style identifies your church's pathway: communication style, means of handling change, decision-making process, outreach/assimilation strategies, and approach to conflict resolution."[1] Knowing that churches go about their ministries in very different ways, he lists the following eight different types of personalities among churches.

Are you an "expressive" church? An expressive church is known by its "exuberant ministry style that is fun-filled, people-focused and activity-oriented."

Are you an "adventurous" church? For these churches, life is one exciting adventure after another!

Are you an "organizer" church? Do you have high expectations of yourself regarding "efficient and timely delivery of programs"?

Are you a "strategizer" church? Do you as a church generally "focus on ministry projects that require thorough research and structured plans leading to clear outcomes in order to move the ministry forward"?

Are you an "entrepreneurial" church? These churches "desire to grow closer to God and to other people, and learn how to practically live in relationship to God through Christ."

Are you a "relational" church? These are the "effective long-range planners that can easily see the potential effects of an idea, program, or service on reaching people for Christ."

Are you an "inspirational" church? This is a "people-to-people" ministry that is sustained by personal contact and is quite "open to accepting new and different people."

Are you a "fellowship" church? These are churches that are "gifted at helping and serving people…they develop well-organized ministries that are coordinated in working toward a better life spiritually, socially and physically for themselves and their community."

These descriptions may help you to know your church much better and can serve foundationally in launching into a new greeters' ministry or can help in revamping a fledgling one.

We've been told through myriad generations to "put your best face/foot forward," along with admonitions about first impressions. It is not easy to translate such personal thoughts or behaviors into ministry at the church, but, regardless of the outcome, such questions require consideration.

Some leaders might consider a greeters' ministry as superfluous or an idea nouveau in Christian ministries today. Deeper consideration about the movement of one's congregation on any given Wednesday or Sunday might ignite a sense of benefit and importance to developing a specific greeters' ministry.

Each church I researched spoke of the added substance and blessing greeters bring to the lives of members and visitors alike. Visitors need help, directions, and warmth in a new place while members need familiarity, warmth, and often additional bits of information in preparation for worship—if just to put their minds at ease. Members also need affirmation and appreciation, all of which can be dispensed through a greeters' ministry. Greeting them by name and/or by title ("Deacon So-and-So") is recognition they enjoy and that can often boost their spirits as they prepare to worship.

Whether you are an urban or a suburban congregation, it is helpful to realize that ministry begins where people enter your property, which can be minutes to an hour before they enter the sanctuary for worship. In urban churches, locations are often on streets with limited parking space. Therefore most congregants must park on the streets surrounding the church. One pastor is teaching his congregation that ministry begins at the curb, extends into the church, and then reaches out into the community. He agrees that people are energized by being touched with such warmth to the degree that they want to give more of themselves—not less—to the cause and kingdom of Jesus Christ.

How, or whether, a greeters' ministry is developed and structured depends upon those three realities: How do you picture the face of your church? How radical do you want your level of hospitality to be? Where does ministry begin for your church on Sundays?

Is the face of your church the kind, class, and race of the people who attend your church or the quality of ministry in which they engage? The quality of worship and ministry of your church become the face of your church; these are your major identifying characteristics beyond just your name.

Some people might consider the greeters' task to be a nice,

friendly gesture with little depth to it. Others will not discern any importance to it compared with other things needing to be done within the ministry or church family or within the community. Let no one deceive you: there is no unimportant task in the vineyard of the kingdom of our Lord and Savior Jesus Christ! Greeting is not just a superficial effort to make folk feel significant. We never know what gesture of kindness or friendliness, which word of genuine care and affection, how many acts of graciousness will unlock the heart of someone who may not as yet know the Lord. That person might be entering the doors of your church!

Motivation for a Greeters' Ministry

The desire to increase the quality and quantity of hospitality experienced at your church serves as adequate motivation to launch a greeters' ministry, but your desire to make a regular, significant impact upon worshipers' frame of mind before they enter the sanctuary should be sufficient cause to initialize your plan. Creating new opportunities for ministry is always excellent motivation to involve new folk who might not already be involved in other ministries of the church. Upon hearing about a greeters' ministry, many folk have said, "I can do this!" With proper training, they can do it well.

Is your church still uncertain whether to launch your greeters' ministry? Then measure your desire to see your visitors and members week after week. The lower the desire, the more you wait for them to enter your space instead of exuding gladness by venturing into their space to welcome them.

Your greeting is your investment in the soul of all who enter to worship. Your greeting can be the Spirit of Christ reaching through you into the lives of those you encounter. It is a relatively easy task but not one is to be taken lightly. The names are legion of those who have been turned away from the church by a hurtful word, an unintended slight, or a brush-off or because they were ignored or not responded to properly. You do not need to add to that number by not doing your task of greeting well. Be genuinely friendly but with a great level of seriousness about the task.

People need to feel accepted, connected, and cared for today more than ever. People in years past did not expect to be formally welcomed into the church. They went out of duty as well as enjoyment. They went out of their personal need and habit as well as a religious compulsion that would have been offended with a welcome that would have suggested they were doing something out of the norm.

What Would Your Greeters' Ministry Look Like?
Fashioning a greeters' ministry that reflects the character and personality of your church is the task at hand, not to compete with other congregations but to reflect that which is natural to and grounded in the best that your church is ready to offer at its front doors or between the parking lot and sanctuary.

Prepare the Doors
Will you provide the courtesy of having door openers for your arriving worshipers? Will all of your greeters await worshipers only in the narthex? Which doors are key to the arrival of your

worshipers? This will help you to decide not only how many teams you need but also which locations are strategic to greeting arriving worshipers. Is there appropriate carpeting or a non-slip, shoe-cleaning (inclement weather) rug at these doors?

How do you want your greeters to look to your members and visitors? What kind of uniforms will enable them to stand out? Something black and white is basic, but something colorful is far more appealing whether in a stole or a specially made shirt or armband. Any of these will allow your greeters to stand out.

What Style of Greeters' Ministry?

Greeters may be dispersed two or three per door depending upon the size of your congregation and the size of the crowd for any particular service. Have them stratified so that worshipers who walk past your first greeter who is busy greeting another worshiper will not feel left out or ignored but will be noticed by your second greeter...or third. Strategically placing them with some depth will ensure that no entering worshiper is missed or ignored or left to enter worship without having been greeted.

Should your greeters' ministry be family style or all male or all female or mixed? You have some options, and it could vary from Sunday to Sunday. Mix and match your teams in some creative ways.

With the greater variety of churches, many people do not feel compelled to attend a family or community congregation but, rather, any church. Thus, as they enter often unknown spiritual/religious territory, a warm, genuine, welcoming atmosphere is the bonus they need to consider returning. If people are loosely connected to former churches, how can you inspire them to affiliate with your church? I have found that many people attend a church for months, even years, before deciding to join. What finally brings them to a decision is not always what they hear from the pulpit but how they have been made to feel from the moment they walk through the doorway. Creating those kinds of warm moments is the challenge and basic task of your greeters' ministry.

More than that, we should learn the lesson of the Old Testament. As the ancient Jew was a "stranger in a strange land," so we walk a similar path. "This world is not my home, I'm just passing through." Hospitality eases that passage for many. By providing hospitality we proclaim, in a practical sense, that we are pilgrims, not permanent residents (Genesis 18:1-8).

Serving as a greeter is a place where one's faith should shine. We've sung "This Little Light of Mine" nine hundred jillion times, but if there ever was *a* place for that light of faith, hope, and love to shine, it is in the space between the door of the church and the door of the sanctuary. Therefore, in training and in orientation, there should be a constant effort to make faith more applicable to the greeting moment by helping greeters to exude a high level of enthusiasm and excitement about arriving worshipers.

Christian love is not a feeling. Christian love is an attitude born out of a will and determination to do what pleases God and what blesses other people. Enable your greeters to stay focused on the needs of others and not on their own needs and you will be preparing them to serve in a more excellent way.

Measuring Readiness to Serve

Jim Loehr declares that "energy, not time, is the fundamental currency of high performance"[2] and that "performance, health and happiness are grounded in the skillful management of [that] energy."[3] In order for us to "be fully engaged" he states that "we must be physically energized, emotionally connected, mentally focused and spiritually aligned with a purpose beyond our immediate self-interest."[4] He says that "full engagement begins with feeling eager to get to work...[and] equally happy to return home...and capable of setting clear boundaries between the two. It means being able to immerse yourself in the mission you are on."[5] This is key to your effectiveness in serving as a greeter.

It might seem like an easy task, not requiring much brain power to accomplish a smile and a handshake; however, do not be fooled about the amount of energy poured out into the lives of others during your duty as a greeter. Unless you function in a robotic way, many questions and decisions will flow automatically through your mind as you approach worshipers and as they move towards you to be welcomed in appropriate ways. It takes much energy to discern their needs and to react accordingly to those needs.

Challenges and Opportunities

Finding God's purpose in your service to the church is of great importance. Loehr also declares that "purpose fuels performance." Sometimes the simplest tasks can be the most difficult to accomplish! Whether the tasks are simple or complex, Loehr provides a high-octane answer for us in this statement. I heartily add that unless as a greeter you find God's purpose in welcoming people to worship, you might not function at your best or in ways that are warm, kind, and efficient.

Work through your biases. Your congregation may draw folk of various racial or ethnic identities. This fact may place some members in the stress of not knowing how to relate to people of such differences. My experiences—and there have been many over these many years of ministry in forty-two different countries and forty-three of the fifty United States—reveal that the one who is "different" often experiences a sense of isolation or a sense of superficial acceptance. You cannot resolve this whole matter for your church as a greeter, but you can enable those who are ethnically or racially different to experience a genuine welcoming moment as they move towards the sanctuary. In working through any possible biases, you can more effectively do what Gilbert Bilezikian refers to in *Community 101*

> as the most important thing that God is doing in the world…God has one priority project throughout history, one that He will bring to climatic completion at the end of history—the formation of the new community. Since community alone will survive from this world into the next, it is ultimately the only thing God is doing today that has eternal significance.[6]

He adds that "whether community happens or not may not be left to chance. Christians are under obligation to make it happen."[7] "Making it happen" is the effortless way of making the stranger in your midst feel as though he or she is a viable and authentic part of your church community. Partnering with God in your greeters' ministry is to truly know that greeting is not about you. Greeting is about the "stranger," family member, or friend coming into our midst with whom we must create community by the help of the Holy Spirit and under the direction of God's Word.

The ministry of greeting is not about who you are in the church, your social standing in your community, or any demographic that could potentially separate you from folk entering your church doors. Nor is it about who you are not. A lack of a healthy ego can be just as detrimental in the ministry of greeting as too much ego. You are not serving to be in the public eye or to showcase yourself from Sunday to Sunday. Rather, greeting is about the ability to create the experience of another person being warmly accepted without any sense or gesture of deservedness or judgment on your part. When you are spiritually healthy, you have the capacity to give out far more love to other human beings than you ever might need to receive from them.

A Position of Trust

Welcoming God's people is a position of trust. In your duties, you represent the face and spirit of your congregation. Take that position seriously. When people see you at your post, they see the congregation they are entering. Be at your best. "Glad hand" as many people as you can, but you don't have to shake every hand. Let's face it, some people are a bit squeamish about shaking hands due to a level of health consciousness. Though I cannot document this assertion, I imagine that is at least part of the reason why the "fist bump" was started. However, on a personal level, I do not enjoy shaking hands with a greeter who has on gloves, though they are often part of the uniform that the church requires. The only reason—and for me it is a compelling reason—is that it smacks of artificiality. A light touch or tap on the arm or back should also be acceptable. Achieve enough orientation towards the person so that people know they have not been ignored or overlooked.

Be visitor-sensitive. People might be insecure, self-conscious, conspicuous, alone, even afraid that they don't fit in. They are coming to you, but they are looking beyond you trying to get to the sanctuary. They are seeking God most often because they have specific needs. Remember that the major difference between churches is not simply their various characteristics but rather the way they treat their arriving visitors and members.

CHAPTER 4

Organization of the Work

If the purpose of a greeters' ministry is to welcome and provide assistance to those who enter the doors or property of the church, how is that to be effectively achieved? This chapter will provide you with a way to view your entire church facility and family relative to beginning or further establishing a greeters' ministry.

From my observation, the understanding of church membership has changed significantly over the last few decades for practical, emotional, and spiritual reasons. People often travel for miles rather than attend a church in their more immediate community. People are not as tied to the ol' home church as in previous generations; the lure of big-church activities, great singing, and more anointed preaching or teaching have all resulted in more church hopping than in previous generations. Many people have their names on one church roll but attend or are active at another church. Some tend to worship wherever the impulse strikes them, floating sometimes for a few years between visiting and church membership. How are these loosely attached souls to become attached and grow into committed church members? How they are met at your doorways is a great beginning.

Another consideration is that because of the onslaught of technology, people are yet in need of the human touch to feel more accepted, more cared for, and more connected today than ever. In years past, people did not need to be welcomed into the church—it was their church! To extend a welcome in a service was a programmatic function. Members went out of personal need or habit, as well as a religious compulsion that would have been offended with a welcome that would have suggested they were doing something out of the norm. Times have changed!

Proper preparation is paramount. Essential training and orientation are critical to the immediate success and longevity of this ministry of greeting. Jesus sent two disciples ahead of the rest of them to prepare a place and a meal for the group as they were nearing Jerusalem for the last time before the cross.

> On the first day of the Festival of Unleavened Bread, the disciples came to Jesus and asked, "Where do you want us to prepare the Passover meal for You?" "As you go into the city," he told them, "you will see a certain man. Tell him, 'The Teacher says: My time has come, and I will eat the Passover meal with my disciples at your house.'" So the disciples did as Jesus told them and prepared the Passover meal there. When it was evening, Jesus sat down at the table with the twelve disciples. (Matthew 26:17-20 NLT)

Certainly this text refers to the great season and celebration of Passover, when special preparations had to be made. However, do not miss the point of preparation by the few for the many. Jesus sent two disciples ahead of the rest of them to prepare, which signals the quality of hospitality needed, desired, and planned. The levels of planning and preparation are obvious for a quality of hospitality to be enjoyed by all at what we refer to as the Last Supper.

Hospitality is more than a warm, friendly smile and a firm handshake from a greeter as worshipers make their way into the sanctuary. Minimal to significant preparation must be made depending upon the condition of the entrance areas that will be covered and the amount of time needed to address matters of budget, leaders, and authority for this ministry. What are some of the clear indicators that ensure a greeters' ministry is ready to be launched? Assessing the responses to the following considerations might prove beneficial to your preparation.

How Ready Are You?

To sufficiently assess your readiness, you might want to review what improvements, if any, need to be made to your entrances and/or your narthex for the comfort of your visitors and members, including what aesthetic value could be added. If the changes are structural, including new paint, flooring, or carpeting, then proper budgetary matters would need to be addressed with the trustees.

Seek out the best leaders you can find: someone or a few folk ready to take on the responsibility of working to recruit a large enough team.

Discern the number of church entrances at which it is best to place greeters. Choose to focus initially only on the main entrance if you prefer.

Discern an appropriate ratio of greeters to worshipers.

Select a rotation cycle; for example, whether greeters will serve one or two Sundays a month. This rotation will dictate the number of greeters required to staff this ministry.

Consider one to three families with children (preferably ages seven to eighteen) who are known for their hospitality and who might provide leadership initially.

Ask whether the pastor is willing to support and encourage this new level of hospitality that will bless the congregation.

Here are some clear indicators of your readiness:

> A sufficient number of volunteers have signed up.
> Training has been organized and/or completed.
> The main entrance has been meticulously prepared (if needed).
> Appropriate attire has been selected to make greeters easily identifiable.
> Connections have been established regarding whom to contact in emergencies or the need for critical/urgent assistance during greeting times.
> Walkie-talkies have been purchased (if needed).
> Rosters, complete with contact information and Sundays on duty, have been prepared.

With the greater variety of churches that exist today, people do not feel compelled to attend a family church or a community church but rather any church to which they may be drawn for different reasons. Thus, they may enter unknown spiritual or religious territory, and a warm, genuinely welcoming atmosphere is the bonus they need to consider returning or to feel better about attending. This is a key reason for not overloading the greeting moment with handouts, papers of all kinds, or flyers. An occasional gift, as mentioned elsewhere in this book, adds a unique touch on a Sunday of special celebration. Otherwise, handouts of any kind by any greeters should not be given. The information desk should be reserved for these items that are not already included in the bulletin, which they will receive from the usher upon entering the sanctuary. Don't be so eager to present the church to the visitor that you lose sight of warmly welcoming the visitor into worship.

How Ready Are Your Surroundings?

Clear assessment is helpful; an honest appraisal about your entranceways as well as the potential individuals who you might envision joining the greeters' ministry are both paramount considerations. Are you ready as the newly assigned leader of this new ministry to provide an honest appraisal relative to changes that may need to be made before launching into a greeters' ministry? This quality of assessment is critical to launching a ministry that will be effective and successful.

Clean up! Fix up! Spruce up! Shape up! Warm up! Some of these improvements are ongoing; some may be more long-range in your planning. The important consideration is to at least identify any changes that would support a healthy, vibrant greeters' ministry and lend themselves to appealing entranceways into the church. Any and all of these admonitions might be helpful as you honestly assess the areas that surround the entranceways to your church. Keeping in mind the matters of safety, beauty, or ambiance, what you are seeking to do is to create an environment that is easy to be maintained and sustained over time. This may include considering new paint or new lighting fixtures to bring practical or esthetic balance and warmth into these areas. Engaging the appropriate budgetary process and/or the appropriate overseers is paramount to your success as you prepare people to support this new ministry.

Timeliness and sufficient forethought are important to having your greeter teams prepared with umbrella bags when it's raining or ample rugs to wipe feet on when it's snowing to prevent tracking snow into the sanctuary or leaving a trail on which the next person might slip and fall. Give full thought to the well-being of your worshipers entering the church under any weather conditions. Practically and aesthetically, carefully examine that space—positively and negatively. Discern what it has and what it doesn't have. Develop your list of needed and/or desired improvements. Study it to discern what it is saying to you and to the worshipers you expect to enter. I hope your list is quite short! The most important thing is the new level(s) of awareness that process will create for your team and church leaders.

Let your new greeter team help check the exterior of the church as well, especially around the entryways. Since this will be their primary space for ministry, this kind of walk-through will help in their preparation. Do not hesitate to draw in your sexton and other service teams such as parking attendants, because they will need to work together to ensure the best possible greeting experience for your worshipers. Some of the following matters may need to be considered by the greeters.

Safe: Are the areas around your entranceways safe for those entering? Visit those areas with a keen eye not only to the possibility of danger to their safety personally but also from the perspective of ease of entering the church.

Clean: Where best should cleanliness be practiced and considered than in any congregation that loves the Lord, particularly as you are considering better welcoming members and guests? "Because we have these promises, dear friends, let us cleanse ourselves from everything that can defile our body or spirit. And let us work toward complete holiness because we fear God" (2 Corinthians 7:1 NLT).

Cleanliness cannot and should not be allowed to wait until Sunday mornings. Ensure there is great oversight of all of the entranceways so they reflect the quality of cleanliness that should characterize our lives as well as our church. A lack of cleanliness is suggestive of a lack of care and inherent disorder. Neither of these speaks well for any Christian church, which should always be trying to do its best for the Lord as well as for one another. First Corinthians 12:25 tells us to "care for each other" (NLT). A part of that caring is appropriate preparation, whether in our homes or in our churches. We are encouraged as well to "abound in love to one another" (1 Thessalonians 3:12 NKJV).

Free of clutter: I have been in numerous churches over thirty years of ministry, and I am still amazed about where they choose to store some things. Consider whether your church might need additional storage space if previously you have used hallways for storage after closets were filled. Do some items need to be sorted out, discarded, or relocated to better storage areas of the church? Like individuals, congregations tend to hold onto things no longer needed—and some things that are beyond repair but have not been discarded as yet. Free your church of clutter, and feel the relief as you prepare to more warmly welcome the members you have and new members as well.

Inviting: How do you add warmth to your home? How does one make empty space more inviting? What can you do to your entranceways to create the sense of being appealing and engaging to those arriving? A few items that come to mind are flags or banners—both decorative and/or those announcing information. Colorful floral arrangements are always appropriate.

There is usually great artistic talent within most congregations. Start with the children: let them draw pictures on a biblical theme, then purchase some inexpensive frames and have your own art exhibit. The children would be thrilled, and parents would be proud of such a display. Expensive art is not necessary, but a bit of color is always inviting to the eye.

For convenience, a few nice chairs for those whose trek from where they parked the car was a bit strenuous or for those who have been let off while a friend or spouse parks the car would be appropriate. Comfort is important and considerate for such individuals.

Check out the paint on the walls in your entranceways. Perhaps the color needs to be changed, or wonderful biblical passages about hospitality could be stenciled on the walls in a few places. Again, coordinate all appropriate ministries and authorities to accomplish these ends.

Consider the physical comfort of worshipers. If possible, the temperature of entranceways should be a minimum of 5 to 10 degrees different from the temperature outside. People entering the church should experience a noticeable difference as they are being welcomed. Imagine the feeling of stepping into warmth after walking through chilly rain, or coolness on a warm, humid day. Reasonable attention to comfort is another way to welcome folk. If necessary, make this part of your long-term planning, and cooperate with leaders regarding finances.

Lighting: The importance of lighting is impossible to over-emphasize. There needs to be sufficient light to allow for ease of walking. Yet, too much light can be glaring and uninviting to those entering even from sunlight. A medium level of electric light balanced with the light from windows and doorways in your narthex is important to consider. There is no need to go overboard with new lighting; just add a lamp or two in appropriate places if necessary, again to keep the entrance areas bright.

Signs: Have appropriate directional signs—everyone in need should not have to ask the location of your bathrooms. On this point, you will want to indicate facilities for worshipers who may have physical challenges. Or, if you have family bathrooms, it's helpful for people to know that. (Think of a parent who may have a baby needing a diaper change; you would not relish having to search for a changing station, and neither do other worshipers.) Easily visible signs are most helpful to your greeters as well as to your worshipers.

Vary your signs of welcome—utilize some permanent and some temporary signs to inform, invite, and inspire entering worshipers.

You have succeeded in making your entranceways more hospitable if you have accomplished the following:

> removed any and all obstacles
> made the place easily accessible, especially for people with disabilities
> monitored the temperature
> discerned the needs of your guests
> discerned ways to make the space more convenient and comfortable

How Ready Are Your Greeters?

You have assessed the quality of your church's facilities. Now, fill those entrance spaces with the warmth of human caring, and you are sure to win the hearts of those arriving. You will not need to tell them you care; they can see it even before you offer to them any words of welcome. Light up these spaces with your smiles and the genuineness of your affection toward those who are coming to worship the Lord. The Apostle Peter gives us pertinent advice: "greet one another" (1 Peter 5:14) and "offer hospitality to one another" (1 Peter 4:9).

So that your greeters provide members and visitors with the quality of hospitality you desire, you'll want to set out the following guidelines. To launch and/or to train new recruits, a minimum of two six-hour sessions should be considered. This training should cover the following subject matter. (More information about training and structure can be found in the appendix to this book.)

Attire. Ushers need to be in uniform because they are the go-to people when worshipers need information and/or direction. In a large or formal church, it may be useful for greeters also to wear uniforms, but remember that a person in uniform may seem less welcoming. Greeters do not necessarily need uniforms, although some churches require white shirts and black skirts or pants, and others require white gloves. In many churches, usual church clothes are acceptable for greeters.

Some teams use armbands, pins, or badges. Another option is a colorful sash or shoulder stole indicating that a person is a greeter. It should say "Greeter" or "Welcome," whichever is preferable. Either would convey the message of warmth that you are there to offer.

Shoes should be at the individual's discretion; comfort is more important than uniformity. Remember that you are not attempting to make your greeters' attire uniform, just welcoming, and appropriate.

Familiarity with the entire church structure. Take a couple of church tours to ensure that your greeters are thoroughly acquainted with all that is open and available to your worshipers during services and between. Few things are as frustrating to a new person as needing to ask several people for directions in the church before he or she can get the information needed.

Familiarity with church events. Know what's happening in your church. Review the bulletin regularly. Check the church website. Put church events on your personal calendar to stay advised.

Familiarity with the visitors' desk. Know where it is and what it handles from week to week because some duties can change.

Entrance assignments. You may have a permanent post, but your team leader may decide upon a rotational system that does not allow you to serve at only one post all the time. Keep a copy of your schedule handy. Have it posted in a permanent place so that others without a handy personal copy may check it to ensure that they are serving at the correct post.

Time commitment. People will be able to make varying commitments of time. If possible, let no one serve more than two Sundays a month for their well-being and to allow for sharing the opportunity with more of your members. When you have some people with very limited time available, ask them to serve for a specific amount of time (three months perhaps); then they know that this particular service to the congregation ends when that time is up. This might help in gaining some seasoned members.

Rotational schedule. Ideally, each team serves one Sunday a month. Marry your teams to specific standard Sundays such as more youth on Youth Day, fathers on Father's Day, mothers on Mother's Day, etc.

Team assignments based on preferred Sundays. Folk do have other commitments at your church, as well as family or work commitments. Therefore, allow them to choose their Sunday, thus preventing additional stress and making it easier to recruit and retain them in the greeters' ministry.

Monthly meetings at the beginning. Then morph into bi-monthly or even quarterly meetings once you discern that the team has jelled to a great degree and many of the kinks of launching a ministry have been worked out, questions have been answered, and training is complete. Use a bit of drama in your meetings to emphasize an important point for your greeters.

Accountability. You shouldn't need to babysit greeters. Lay out your expectations, discuss them, and agree upon them with the understanding of the individual responsibility each greeter bears, such as securing his or her replacement or substitute for a given shift on the Sunday served. This should occur whether the absence is known well in advance or on short notice. The team should not be hampered because of failure of notice. You cannot overemphasize this. To make it less important is to undermine the cohesiveness of your team.

Checklists. Checklists ensure that memory is better served and requirements are met. The checklist harnesses the team and creates a level of confidence. Provide a permanent space for orienting your greeters. Put reminders there, along with the normal assignment/rotation grid. Remind greeters of people's allergies— no cologne! Remind them of their personal hygiene. Remind them of their personal spiritual preparation to ensure a more spiritual frame of reference as they are greeting worshipers.

Belligerent or upset worshipers. First deal with the problem to the best of your ability. Calm the person. Call your team leader if necessary. When all is calm, refocus the person toward worship— recasting that worshiping posture while maintaining your own.

In all circumstances, remember that you are the disciple that Jesus has sent ahead on the journey to "prepare for those on the way." By keeping in mind the focus of your ministry—to welcome members and visitors as children of God—you follow Jesus' example and make people feel truly welcome in your church.

CHAPTER 5

Before and After the Service

The fundamental decision that will shape every element of preparation and service of greeters are the decisions about the levels of service to be offered—individually and collectively—to the arriving worshipers. These are not just your friends and family and community folk, members and visitors coming to your church. Whichever of these categories they might fall into, they are all in one category only: they are God's people. Understanding and integrating such a reality into every area of your service as greeters will make the key difference in the quality of duties performed. Be fairly warned: one thought less than this, and you might begin to reduce the level of dignity, warmth, and respect you could bring to the task of greeting.

Successful churches steep their greeters in a noble perspective. About its greeters, one church (New Birth Missionary Baptist Church, Atlanta) declared that "we are the welcoming arm of the corporate ministry…and you are submitted to the vision and visionary" of your church. This beautifully frames the greeter's task relative to their necessary preparation, which includes

- nurturing greeters biblically
- energizing a team spirit

- calling out the best in them
- sensing their readiness/giftedness to serve
- communicating pertinent information
- coaching in problem areas
- polishing their techniques
- focusing toward the task

Before the Service

It is essential to be prepared fully before the first worshipers arrive. In your pre-service team meeting, posts will be confirmed, new posts assigned if necessary, pertinent information disseminated, and questions about the day answered. Some teams prefer to assign permanent posts while others rotate their greeters to enable them to learn the fuller line of responsibilities. The first can be justified for a set time, but no greeter should ever be allowed to marry a post or think that he or she cannot serve where needed. Serving where needed is essential in developing levels of leadership and flexibility. If wheelchairs need to be rolled out of the closet and into place along with other guest-welcoming needs and/or accessories, such tasks should be assigned in the meeting or taken care of by the head greeter prior to that meeting so that placement can be announced and confirmed with those on duty. It is necessary for your leader to be fully informed about the day's important church announcements and with whom or where worshipers might need to go to connect once the service is over. Appropriate directions are essential in the service of your members and visitors rather than their having to ask various people and hearing "I don't know!" Planning details are the bedrock of pre-service meetings.

Mandatory meetings prior to and following worship are basic aspects of your ministry to the church. In too many churches today, greeting is taken as one of the more mundane tasks within congregational life, and therefore insufficient seriousness is given to the vital need for preparation and post-worship evaluation or debriefing. A team approach has begun to emerge within many greeter ministries, and that team approach sets the level of accountability to which the group will aspire.

Sports teams start together and return to the locker room together for closure before going on about their personal lives after the game. No team takes the field without a huddle, which is critical to each teammate knowing the game plan for *that* day, not a recollection from the previous game. No team dismisses from the field—and it's not just about showering and changing clothes. Team spirit and closure are just as important as pre-game preparation. Start together and end together. Manage the time to keep it focused, short, and sweet. Willow Creek's ministry leaders suggest that we send greeters home full of compliments or great visitor vignettes from the day and a constant orientation to the vision and goal of their service: a level of excellence to the glory of God and the blessedness of the worshipers they serve.

Few churches have space for a designated greeters' room. When and where that is possible, the congregation can be better served and greeters can be better organized in their weekly efforts. However, when that is not available, the work and meetings must go on in some appropriate manner. It is essential to have a ground zero where greeters can meet uninterrupted and can leave their personal belongings as they prepare to mount their posts. If that space is not available to you now, seek to create it if at all possible, even if it's just an area that can be screened off with a portable screen. Include a full-length mirror and a cabinet of some kind that can be locked. Keep extra copies of your greeters' manuals for easy reference plus several Bibles for more extended devotional times during monthly or quarterly meetings. It is recommended that devotions used prior to mounting of posts are printed on cards that can be slipped into pockets for quick reference if a pick-me-up is needed while on duty. Such devotionals are easily printed and prepared well in advance by a designated person.

Leaders of the team should help newer team members achieve serving satisfaction, which will allow them to offer better service and ensure greater joy in the service they will be trained to offer. This touches on appropriate mentoring. Suffice it to say that people do not learn only from initial training; they need to be taken under someone's wing and oriented to the quality of service to which you want them to aspire, which surpasses the basics of greeting they learned during training. In their training, they learn the practice of greeting; however, from their mentor they catch the spirit of hospitality.

Pre-service meetings facilitate opportunities to gain updated information that will be important to disseminate to worshipers if asked and to be reminded of important church information that greeters should be able to answer without hesitation. "I don't know" is an inadequate response in this gatekeeping ministry. That is the coldest, emptiest customer service response ever be offered to a seeker. It devalues the honest inquiry of the seeker and puts the greeter in an uncaring light. If the person is a visitor, such a response might inhibit him or her from returning to a place where those appointed to welcome and assist did not seem to care enough to have the necessary information for visitors. The lack of preparation may communicate a degree of indifference that becomes a stumbling block rather than a stepping stone to help the new worshiper experience God more fully and connect more intimately with your community of faith.

In writing this book, I interviewed the trainer of all employees of a successful grocery chain. The owners of the chain had started out with barely 500 feet of sales space in their first store, and now this family-owned grocery chain is spread across three different states with numerous locations within each state. Ukrops has often been ranked nationally not just because of their bottom line but especially because of the quality of their customer service. Young, retired, and physically challenged employees don't just carry your groceries to your car; they engage you in meaningful conversation on the way. Ask any little question in the store, and the person to whom you addressed the question can reply promptly—without seeking out one to five other employees to find the answer. Ask where to find a product, and you are not just directed to the correct aisle—you are escorted directly there. This quality of customer care is grounded in the owners' religious faith, which they have publicly affirmed throughout the years. When Virginia allowed stores to be open on Sunday and to sell alcoholic beverages, Ukrops said a resounding no to both. The training they provide every employee underscores the reality that our faith as Christians should allow us anywhere—but particularly in the church—to have the warmest, most genuine encounters of all as we fulfill our tasks of service.

Concentrate on being courteous. Rehearse courteous and thoughtful words and deeds in your mind. Don't hesitate to extend and even overextend yourself to any worshiper in your efforts to ensure that his or her needs have been met. Anticipate worshipers' needs that you might be required to attend to during your time of greeting. This will keep you alert and require you to be knowledgeable not only of the church plant but also of church activities and church leaders with whom you may be required to connect to meet some need(s) of a worshiper.

You are investing your practical and spiritual capital in worshipers, whether they are members or visitors. Keep in mind Psalm 103:4b (NKJV): "Who crowns you with lovingkindness and tender mercies." You are in the position to pass on what you have received from the Lord, who is "merciful and gracious, slow to anger and abounding in mercy" (Psalm 103:8-9 NKJV). Little should make you angry, and your aim prayerfully will be to dispense the mercy that has so filled you.

After the Service

Post-service meetings are encouraged and should be brief—approximately ten minutes—to capture and share what Willow Creek refers to as GEMs (Guest Experience Moments). Often there are those moments on any given Sunday when a special encounter with a worshiper has occurred. Sharing this on the day of occurrence not only brings closure to the day's experience but also helps to build and solidify the team spiritually by further validating the beauty and magnitude of its service.

Post-service meetings also provide an opportunity to deal with matters of discipline while they are fresh in the experience of the greeters. Delay dilutes not only the seriousness of the matter but also teachability about the issues involved. These post-service moments help to elevate clear expectations that emerge out of GEMs with a more celebratory or a more noble perspective. Positive reinforcement is paramount rather than critical examination or interrogation, which makes some people uncomfortable and becomes discouraging to those who seek to serve. Sharing these GEMs in a post-service gathering helps the team to sharpen its skills by assessing how team members could have handled a situation differently or better. Lengthy discussion is not advised. Deal quickly and effectively with the matter(s), but save discussion around the issues raised for your formal monthly meeting or perhaps incorporate them into future training sessions.

Gathering for a few minutes after the service will allow greater coordination relative to those who might be absent the next time of service. Checking in with all members is a valuable way to sustain care and continuity, both of which strengthen the greeters' ministry. Debriefing is essential to maintaining the highest standards in your service. Some greeters may consider a matter that occurred while they served too small to mention. During debriefings, accentuate the fact that no matter is too small or too insignificant to be brought into this moment. This demonstrates a wonderful and needed level of care by the team leader for each greeter. Each greeter, not just his or her service, is valuable to the team. Debriefing is a way of not letting problems accumulate and of ensuring that things needing to be changed are changed while they are new and before they escalate into more major problems. This also is where good coaching can emerge by focusing on "the right way to…" or "the best way to…" without pointing at anyone's failure to meet or uphold the standards to which greeters have agreed.

Joyous happenings that are unshared are greatly reduced in value next week. Difficulties of the day that greeters have experienced that are left hanging for another week or more can fester and even gradually erode confidence in the leader. Likewise, team spirit is potentially diminished, as well as the value of what has been achieved. Your greeters do not need to take negative feelings home with them to affect their life after church. Even if the team leader's response is only, "That's quite a weighty matter. I promise you that we will take this up in our next meeting where it can adequately be dealt with," that matter is diffused. Over…done with in fifteen seconds! The greeter was valued and cared for in the moment! A negative matter was not allowed to fester from lack of attention.

Greeters are encouraged to look realistically at the full amount of time they are giving to the Lord in service on their assigned Sunday. Dashing in and dashing out of church moments before and immediately after worship is not acceptable for a serious team of greeters. Make appropriate plans with your family members or friends on the Sundays you serve so that nothing will interfere with your complete service to the task. This, too, is a test relative to the quality of one's commitment and service not just to the group, not just to the church, but unto the Lord. It is a test relative to whether folk fully comprehend the power and impact of their greeting.

Too often greeters may be so focused on getting out of the church and on with their personal agendas that they almost leave with the worshipers. Your genuine hospitality must extend to seeing your guests appropriately out the door—saying goodbye in one form or another—rather than simply trying to pick up trash as worshipers leave. Worshipers are far more important than the trash they might leave behind. Their departure is a critical moment of closure to their whole worship experience, and greeters can help to seal into them the glorious experience they have had in worship and that they long to take home with them.

These definite times together in pre- and post-service sessions will build the camaraderie of the group. Growing together facilitates the greater possibility of serving together. You get to know not only one another's idiosyncrasies relative to their functioning as greeters, but also respond with greater ease when you need that other greeter's help at your post. Develop, nourish, expect, and require the pre-service meeting because although you might have the same procedures to follow, the same uniform or code of dress, the same badge, and even the same stated goal, it takes a continuous effort at building the team spirit to serve as one. Do not minimize the value of the post-service gathering. It could and should provide some of the most meaningful moments in the life of the group.

Beyond the Task, Toward Ministry

Someone might ask, "Aren't we taking this greeting stuff a bit too far?" Those who have been greeting or ushering for years might have become so jaded that they are satisfied with having seen few if any improvements. They might wonder whether a smile, handshake, or other appropriate greeting behavior makes any significant difference. Many times we are curious about how others see us, and too often we are helpless to change or adjust our normal behaviors that influence or affect people negatively. Too often we want to say, "Well, that's just me..." But God calls us to be at our best in the Kingdom, and the challenge is uniquely and especially laid at our feet as we attempt to extend a hand and a smile to those who would worship God and to our coworkers who are trying to help us do the task.

Dr. Ann Demarais is the founder of First Impressions, Inc., which is based in New York City with an office in California. Change management is one of her areas of specialty. Demarais's website declares that her organization "helps illuminate the links between specific behaviors and how these behaviors make others think and feel, so that clients may send the messages they intend, and not messages they don't." What she offers prompts the question, "Will anyone experience the positive impact of your service in God's house while you're on duty?" This becomes even more important when we realize that people may not remember what was said to them but they will always remember how they were treated.

Training does not end for a servant. At either the pre- or post-service gathering, training essentials can easily be referred to and refreshed. The vision that was originally cast for the team can also be continuously confirmed to keep greeters sharp and ready for service. Such positive focus coupled with strong standards helps solve problems before situations evolve into major dilemmas for the team. A great team spirit may become your greatest recruitment tool because as members see the beauty of that spirit reflected in your service they will be drawn to it as a place where they, too, would like to offer their time and talents. A problem to be addressed within the team is that most leaders are not strong enough to enforce accountability consistently—they settle and, therefore, roll on with whosoever shows up. That's not acceptable. Covenant together for better service and greater expectations of each other.

Guests will compare your care for the sanctuary and entrances with your potential ability to provide appropriate care for them. Though this might never be verbalized in your hearing, you had best believe that such thoughts are real. The measure of care provided to your section is suggestive concerning the measure of care you have the capacity to offer.

"For everyone to whom much is given, from him much will be required" (Luke 12:48 NKJV). That might sound a little heavy for a greeter, but I would encourage you to reacquaint yourself with the powerful space within which you are placed: between God and those who are making their way to worship him. God requires enthusiasm, exuberance, a great desire, and a passion for excellence of all of his servants, and he rebukes a spirit of slothfulness (Matthew 25:26). No one can demand excellence of you; to the degree that you can, you must demand it of yourself even in ordinary tasks. If not, you might not ever get a shot at the extraordinary! How wasteful to languish in mediocrity, to the detriment of many lives and even more worshipers than you could ever number. If the spirit of excellence is nourished in your greeters during these pre- and post-worship gatherings, you will be sure to fill worshipers with joy and delight as you greet them and direct them into the sanctuary. God expects no less.

I've read John 13:1-7 limitless times over many years, but the new insight that I described in chapter 1—how Jesus' love was expressed through his willingness to perform the most menial of tasks for his disciples—caused me to fall in love with Jesus all over again! I hope you'll do the same so that the measure of our love for one another—as we welcome worshipers—can approximate his love for us.

Might I suggest that you take a moment to describe yourself as a Christian? You will most likely speak of your love and your faith and how much Jesus has done for you. That is all well and good, but he wants to build within you greater and greater and greater capacities to express that love and faith in fellowship with others. Never forget that it was Jesus who said, "I tell you the truth, whatever you did for one of the least of these brothers of mine, you did for me" (Matthew 25:40). If Jesus valued and described the simple giving of "a cup of cold water" (Matthew 10:42), think of the value of a kind word, a smile, a warm handshake as you extend yourself in fellowship with arriving and departing worshipers!

CHAPTER 6

In the Worship Service

The greeter's work is not done when the pastor, liturgist, or worship leader steps up to give the call to worship or cue the choir to begin the opening selection in worship. So when the ushers close the doors for worship to begin, that is no signal for all greeters to depart. If no one else is arriving, some greeters may enter the sanctuary and participate more fully in worship. Seats in the rear of the sanctuary should be reserved for this. Depending upon the number of greeters on duty, your greeter team could be reduced by as much as 50 percent at this time. However, a residual team should remain on duty throughout worship, not only to greet latecomers but to also be of help to those who need to leave worship for one reason or another and might need some assistance.

Once worship has begun—given concerns for safety and security or respect for the worship service now underway—some churches may restrict which doors may be used. Often the inner doors of the sanctuary are also regulated once the service begins. Ushers will usually close the doors at or nearest to the center of the sanctuary. This leaves the option for greeters to adjust their posts accordingly, that is, no longer walking people toward the center aisle(s) of the sanctuary but toward doors to the right and left of the center aisle(s). Those doors may also be temporarily closed depending upon what is occurring in worship, but ushers have their cues as to when to reopen them.

Coordinating with the Ushers

Once the service has begun, coordination between greeters and the head usher is important during the transition. This is to ensure appropriate oversight and proper care for the needs of worshipers. For example, during a communion service, greeters may be asked to assist in traffic control, requesting that latecomers wait in the narthex or lobby until an appropriate moment in the service. If there is a baptism or child dedication on a given Sunday, greeters may be asked to direct late-arriving family and

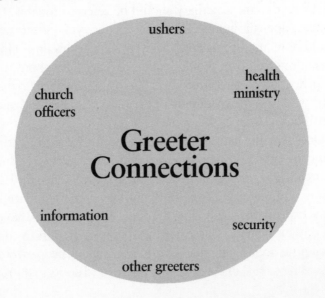

friends to a specific section. On a Sunday when the sanctuary is filled to capacity, the head usher may need to notify the greeters and request their help with directing latecomers to an overflow seating area.

Whatever the specific situation at a particular service, as a greeter, you should rely on the ushers to keep you informed about what is happening inside the sanctuary so that you can do your part in ensuring that the service proceeds decently and in order. That will involve assisting in the smooth and minimally disruptive integration of latecomers or others who must reenter the sanctuary for various reasons during the course of the worship service. Greeters serve as contact points with people in other ministries, as well as with members and visitors (see figure at the left).

Ministry to Latecomers

Although most of your worshipers are probably inside the sanctuary, there will still be a significant number who are struggling to arrive—albeit after the sanctuary doors have closed. After the flow of worshipers slows to a trickle or service begins, make it an official aspect of the greeters' responsibility to pray for worshipers you are serving that Sunday. Pray for their safety, and pray for their spiritual openness.

This is a great opportunity for the team leader to check with greeters to ensure that all is well. While they are on duty is the best time for the team leader to give them a word of encouragement or perhaps to rejoice together over some encounter with a worshiper or some element of service they have experienced that day. Let the following verse inform the service that you offer:

"And whatever you do, work at it with all your heart, as working to the Lord, not for men, since…it is the Lord Christ you are serving" (Colossians 3:23-24). This will help to keep your team members focused, remaining in their role throughout the service and beyond.

In the moments before the service begins, most greeters are aware of their need to smile or at least to attempt to demonstrate an outward appearance of gladness to be in the house of the Lord. After all, there is an obvious audience in those minutes when most worshipers are arriving. However, don't lose your capacity to smile even after most of the crowd has entered the sanctuary. Stragglers definitely need your welcoming smile as much as the first hundred—and perhaps even more so! Any number of obstacles or challenges may have hindered their punctual arrival: a flat tire, a traffic accident, a sick child, a disagreement with a spouse, a wardrobe malfunction, a late bus or train. As a greeter, take the "better late than never" posture and greet latecomers with a full measure of warmth and pleasure in their presence.

The normal, natural eye reveals certain details about those you will encounter. Our socialization provides another lens through which we peer at others, and then our inner spiritual condition will have a profound impact upon how we size up folk we intend to help. Unless you have worked on viewing people objectively, the way you view worshipers entering church has more to do with how you have been socialized by culture than your spiritual capabilities at the time. You will need due diligence in order to change those thoughts and ways of reacting to people.

This is vital because the last worshiper entering is just as important as the first. Although worship has begun, your role and function as a greeter has not yet ended. Those persons should be extended the same warmth, graciousness, and courtesy as did those who arrived on time.

As a practical matter, it would be good for greeters to have a few bulletins outside of the sanctuary especially for the latecomers. Latecomers could be told, "One moment, they're praying now," but they should also be able to follow along with the order of service until they have the opportunity to enter.

So, greeters, stay attuned to where the service is via a well-positioned monitor or speakers. Know the ushers' expectations for seating latecomers, and be attuned above all to how you can best assist people to enter into God's presence through worship.

Assistance for Worshipers with Immediate Personal Needs

People need to experience your interest in them not just as a new member but as a real person. Your one-on-one opportunity with a few folk each Sunday during service can allow them to experience the depth of your hospitality. When someone comes out of worship, approach that person, identify yourself as a greeter, and offer help, assistance, or information.

Engage in focused conversation: "I hope you have enjoyed worship so far." (It might be good for the greeter to briefly comment on any aspect of the worship that blessed worshipers, if you could hear it at your post.)

Offer to wait for the person, and then walk back to the sanctuary with him or her.

Should, perchance, you have no folk in your area during worship, stay in your role as greeter. It is not the time to begin thinking about your dinner at home, or your plans after church, or your job next week, or the distractions of personal challenges in your life. Instead, you might meditate on the scriptural references about the delight in serving as a gatekeeper in the house of the Lord. Stay in your role because you do not know when the next worshiper might pop through that door needing your help. You want to meet that need and not be caught off guard. You are there *for* them!

On most Sundays, you can expect to have several worshipers leave the sanctuary during service to attend to personal needs. Greeters, this is your opportunity to shine and more greatly personalize your care of these worshipers who may not know their way around your facilities. Don't just tell them, "Down the hall and to your left!" Escort them most of the way until you can say, "It's right there on your left." These are strong reasons for you to stay in your role. You are on duty until either you have been appropriately dismissed by your team leader or until the last worshipers have departed the outer doors of the church.

Emergency facilities should be available and unlocked, with appropriate people on duty (e.g., nurse, medic, person experienced in CPR and other emergency kinds of services, even a go-to person who will immediately call 911). Someone's life could be in your hands. This aspect of the greeters' tasks should be well rehearsed and not taken for granted!

Parents may not know of the church's childcare facilities. Therefore, should they need to leave worship because of a crying baby or disruptive child, you may need to show them to the right room or (depending upon the weather) help to take the child outdoors for a moment of fresh air to help calm him or her. The ladies' or family restroom at your church may have a baby-changing station. If it does not, know exactly where to direct a caregiver so that she or he can properly take care of the baby's needs.

Greeters should be able to see the effect their initial greeting and subsequent ministry has had upon worshipers. With hearts being warmed at the entrances to the church, that warming of hearts should become evident in myriad ways in the sanctuary. Worshipers become bearers of greater spiritual vitality when their welcome and the worship service manifest God's loving care.

Maintaining a Worshipful Attitude

The quality, or lack thereof, of the help you will offer to people during worship will depend in part upon where you are mentally, emotionally, and spiritually. If your church is fitted with great technical capability, you should be able to see or at least hear the service in session. Worship! Though you are outside the doors of the sanctuary, worship anyway by staying focused on the progression of the service. Simply because you are on duty does not excuse you from worshiping. Remain in that worship mode. You and your ministry as a greeter will maximize the greater benefit as a result.

On any given Sunday, you may or may not have anyone needing your assistance during worship. Again, stay in your role as a greeter even via planned meditation. There are many studies about the fruit of the Spirit (Galatians 5:22-23). Because nine are listed, I find most often that I have to remind folk that there is no "s" on "fruit," meaning that all nine of these qualities are simultaneously present in you to one degree or another when you have the Spirit of Jesus Christ.

Each quality is vital in your ministry of greeting: love, joy, peace, patience, kindness, goodness, faithfulness, gentleness, and self-control. Learn them. Recite them to yourself. The New Testament is replete with verses that remind us that Christianity is a faith based on love, not hatred or contempt; it's a religion full of joy, not sadness, so it is no wonder that these two qualities would be listed first.

All of the words in this listing are quite easily understood, but I thought it might be helpful to contrast the greater difference between "kindness" and goodness because in English language they are virtually synonymous. In the New Testament, "kindness" often refers to the blessed acts of God that we have experienced, which therefore should be or become a natural part of one's Christian character. "Goodness" seems to express a more practical demonstration, suggesting being orderly, serviceable, and benevolent.

Faithfulness is advised not only in your participation and greeter rotation but also in the qualities your role as greeter requires. At no point during and/or surrounding the worship experience does anyone need harshness. Gentleness is the order of the day emanating from the heart of a servant. Last on this list is self-control, which is not to make it the least important but rather to declare that because you have all the rest of these blessed, beautiful, God-given qualities, you are being reminded that you have the power to require of yourself far beyond what any other person might require of you. You have the last word about your own actions.

Ministry to Exiting Worshipers

Some worshipers must leave the service before the benediction because of their work schedule or some other commitment. When the greeter sees a worshiper departing early, at least inquire if everything is all right if no other needs are evident or have been expressed by the worshiper. On hearing that all is well, offer the person a reason to come back. Say, "So glad you came!" or "Worshiping first will help your workday go better now!" or "I trust that you were blessed by the service!" or at least "Hope to see you next Sunday!"

As church begins to close, the benediction is pronounced and a closing song has been sung. Gradually folk begin to file out, often more hurriedly than when they arrived. A rousing "See you next week!" with a handshake is fine. But more than projecting seven days down the calendar, I suggest that you stay in the moment of anything pertinent to the present moment:

- "Glad you came today!"
- "Hope you were blessed by the service!"
- A phrase from the benediction that is most often said: "The LORD bless thee, and keep thee: The LORD make his face shine upon thee, and be gracious unto thee: The LORD lift up his countenance upon thee, and give thee peace" (Numbers 6:24-26 KJV).
- "The peace of the Lord be with you today!" (Note: In higher liturgical churches, the peace is passed during worship.)

- "The Lord has smiled on you!"
- A phrase from the closing song could also be appropriate: "God be with you!"

Any of these phrases help to seal in what people have already heard and keep you and your greeter task a seamless part of their worship experience.

Before Going Off Duty

As mentioned above, some or all of your team of greeters may be released from duty at a certain point in the service. Whether this is immediately upon the call to worship, when the offering is taken, or later, take the time to look around and assess the physical condition of your station before you leave your post. This might be the time for putting away umbrella-bag stands and removing any other items that were brought out for the convenience of those entering worship. Chairs may now be returned to their rightful places, unless they are deemed permanent in their placement in your entranceway.

Be sure to notice any trash in your area and take the time to pick it up. This not only ensures the tidiness of the entrance but also prevents anyone from tripping over items that could have been easily removed. This low-traffic period may also provide an opportunity to look around for personal items that worshipers may have dropped or left lying around in their rush to enter the sanctuary. Any greeters who are released from duty might take responsibility for collecting such misplaced or forgotten items and turning them in to the church's lost-and-found area, whether that means handing them to the head usher or dropping them at the information desk or wherever your congregation will think to inquire.

While it may be tempting to rush through these steps in your hurry to enter the sanctuary or to leave for home, take your time. Be intentional and thorough. You are beginning to prepare your post for next week's service—leaving it the way you would like to find it the next time. What's more, you are also ensuring that exiting worshipers leave with a final impression of a well-cared-for house—and not with a wake of cast-off items and litter. Remember that not only beauty but also cleanliness becomes the Lord's house.

I recently met a newly called pastor who shared that virtually his first task was to take the leaders of his congregation on a weekend retreat with the intention of not only shaping a vision but also focusing the ministry they, together, would expect to have. I was awed by the fact that this group of leaders cited five things that would characterize their ministry as a church congregation; however, I was more greatly awed by hearing they had listed as their first priority "radical hospitality" as the defining quality of every ministry of the church. They saw this as critically important and enabling them to become effective servants within the kingdom. Greeters, your task is where radical hospitality begins!

CHAPTER 7

Common Challenges in the Work

As with any other ministry of the church, the greeter ministry faces its share of challenges. Unlike many more traditional and established ministries, however, the work of the greeter may be questioned or scoffed at in its most basic premise. Some church members will not see the need for a formal ministry devoted to the fundamental task of welcoming people into the church. Some folk assume that this role can be fulfilled by the ushers; others will propose that it is the responsibility of every church member to offer a warm welcome to any individual who enters the church. A few may question the need to offer a welcome at all.

By now, I trust we have established that such sentiments are neither biblical nor historical in the traditions of the universal Christian church. And while a small congregation may choose to train its ushers to function in a dual role as greeters as well, it has been my experience that it is preferable to have even a small team of individuals dedicated to the task of greeting worshipers and assisting their entry into the facility and the fellowship of the service.

Responding to Resistance

You can employ two strategies in response to those who resist your efforts to establish, develop, and maintain a greeter ministry: actively educate and passively overlook. Central to both strategies, however, is effective communication. Just as you communicate to recruit, you will also need to communicate to overcome resistance. Your clear articulation concerning the ministry's purpose, parameters, and priorities will be critical for its development, validation, and survival.

Communicate Through Education

Bible studies on hospitality and on the purpose of greeting are paramount in preparing a congregation to move toward such a ministry. Those who will be recruited for the greeters' team need it to prepare to offer such ministry. However, those who will be greeted need it as well to appreciate its practice, presence, and power to help open people spiritually to the worship experience they are about to enter. It will even transform some who would enter the church unprepared to worship. Members need to know this in order to value a greeters' ministry and hold it in the high esteem it deserves: that greeting is not a New Age thing but is biblically grounded in God's expectations of us.

Educating any congregation begins in the pulpit. If the pastor is not sold on the idea, espousing some level of commitment to it and regularly advocating for it from the pulpit, then the road to success will be difficult at best or impossible at worst. If the pastor does not launch the idea of a greeters' ministry, and it originates from the pew instead, be certain to obtain his or her blessing. Offer insight into the significant ongoing educational and supportive roles that need to be provided from the pulpit. This is the beginning of educating your congregation.

Commitment to Bible study on the subject is also vital if the congregation is to have a well-rounded awareness and sensitivity to what the ministry of greeting is all about. "The Pastor's Page" in the bulletin is also a powerful educative tool catching those who may not attend Bible study. Some topics for both might include

> "Hospitality from a Biblical Perspective"
> "Greeting Is More Than a 'Hello!'"
> "Strangers in Our Midst"
> "Understanding the Tabernacle"
> "Love…Grace…Mercy…Joy…Doesn't Stop
> with Me…It Starts!"

Part and parcel of educating via the pulpit is also an element of recruiting in that standards and expectations of excellence can be well established through the pastor, freeing recruitment from "just friends" or pulling in anyone available. This would include (in some teaching moments) the qualities desired and the training available for greeters.

Knowing the power of a good marketing campaign, I would suggest that a comprehensive plan be put in place for a month to launch a greeters' ministry. Part of your marketing strategy should be to keep ads and announcements brief. Here are a few good themes:

■ Bring a Smile…We'll Make It Last!
■ God Needs a Few Good Greeters!

- Like Meeting Folk? Come Meet a Few Hundred!
- Navy Seals Swim with Sharks! Combat Soldiers Fight in Strange Places! God's Army Is Still Waiting to Be Mobilized! READY?
- Feeling a Little Shy These Days? Join the Greeters' Ministry, We'll Get You out of That!

The pulpit lifts up the vision for ministry, orients the people toward its accomplishment, and provides the underlying knowledge necessary for sustaining vital ministries of the church. The greeters' ministry team should plan and execute appropriate training modules, develop strategies for ministry, and decide the location and rotation of teams along with providing ongoing inspiration to serve. Beyond the foundational aspects with team members in regularly scheduled meetings, the following topics are crucial around which to build an educative framework:

- Nurturing a Team Spirit
- The Difference Between a Grin and a Smile
- Cultivating Genuine Church Fellowship Through Hospitality
- Warming Up to God's People
- Evangelism Is Winning the Lost; Greeting Is Keeping Them!

I grew up in a church where even the welcome in worship and programs printed in the bulletin would elicit the ire and negative comments of a few of our more verbal older members. They could not see the need of welcoming people into God's house, declaring that "they ought to know they are welcome!" That always amazed and saddened me. While nothing ever stopped such negativity, fortunately nothing ever stopped other people from sharing many beautiful, creative welcomes to visitors during the many church programs.

If you encounter any strong resistance to the importance of greeter ministry, remind people that the Bible is replete with gracious hospitality of God from Genesis to Revelation, as demonstrated through many a saint and sinner. It is God's house, but folk see us before they see him—they hear our words of welcome sometimes before they even hear his voice of welcome. God's graciousness is delivered through human instrumentality and personnel.

Communicate Through Overlooking Resistance

Assuming that you have the support of your pastor and other key church leaders, a second strategy for dealing with resistance is a passive one. In conjunction with congregational education, you can take the high road by overlooking resistance in the church. Decline to engage the naysayers. If you are certain of God's calling in establishing or continuing this ministry, be obedient to that calling. Respectfully disregard those who would argue or debate the validity of the vocation.

This strategy demands communication among your team members because if you are to be effective in overlooking resistance, the entire team must be consistent in its refusal to engage in the controversy. Explain to the team your intention to move forward in nonconfrontational obedience to God's call on your life. Invite them to partner with you in fulfilling the role and responsibilities of the greeter—and through your obedient service, as a team you will become a testimony to the value and vocation of the work.

Recruiting New Members

As suggested above, communication is also critical as you tackle the often challenging task of recruiting members for your team of greeters. This task will be more challenging if the ministry is new to your congregation. You may have to include more elements of education in your recruitment materials or presentations—not only for the individuals who will consider signing up but also for congregants who need to know how this new ministry will affect their lives in the church.

Recruiting will be a major challenge unless the role of greeting is sufficiently laid out and differentiated from ushering and information table service. Establish clear boundaries so that the three ministries are not duplicating efforts or unintentionally doing the work of the others. Clear role descriptions and task assignments are necessary to eliminate any and all confusion about what new recruits may expect to do—in general and at any given service.

In your recruitment campaign, you might emphasize that this ministry is one in which any member of the church family may be involved. That makes the ministry of greeting unique in most churches. Nearly every other ministry of the congregation is separated by age or gender. But the gifts that equip a person for the work of the greeter are not limited by gender, age, or even health. Seniors, children, and people with disabilities are all capable of offering a welcome and basic orientation to the service and physical facility. Moreover, an entire family might appreciate the ability to serve in ministry together—parent and child, grandparent and grandchildren, couples at all stages in life. Consider recruiting whole families to service on a single Sunday. It is on-the-job ministry training for children and youth, who learn more effectively by practicing the skills than by observing. Moreover, the enthusiasm that young people bring is infectious for incoming worshipers—and offers parents an opportunity not just to model a servant's heart but to witness such a heart being developed in their offspring. More and more churches are interested in cultivating intergenerational programs, and the work of the greeter is ideally suited for such a family-friendly ministry.

Having greeter teams that feature a mixture of ages, abilities, races, and both genders will enliven your ministry and offer an inviting picture of your congregation's diversity—a diversity that will reflect the variety of people who are entering your church doors. This intergenerational and multicultural approach to team ministry should also increase the level of commitment among your greeters as the presence of children and youth will help to keep the family focused on serving together.

Other Challenges

Need for enrichment. In the humble role of gatekeeper, the volunteer greeter may find the task becoming mundane and ordinary. As a ministry, be creative about enriching the experience for team members. Such enrichment should go beyond teaching and orienting new members to the task. Plan some level of fellowship within the team to enhance greater acquaintance with one another. The better you know one another as team members, the better your quality of service and the stronger each one's level of commitment. Greeters will feel more valued, and thus their ability to value other team members will increase, creating a bond and greater potential for cooperation within the team. Enriching ideas can range from relaxed fellowship in one another's homes to scheduled visits to other churches to expand the team's vision for the scope and function of the ministry. The possibilities are numerous. Just ensure that such enrichment occurs because it will help you build a successful team.

Depersonalization. When a greeter stops seeing individual worshipers and perceives a faceless horde coming in to worship, the heart has gone out of the ministry, leaving greeters just another role to play at church. Such depersonalization can be the result of long service as a greeter; one's heart may grow hard, or one's spirit may grow weary. Guard against burnout of this kind by establishing annual reviews of all team members by the head of the ministry. Such reviews allow the ministry leader to ask questions and share concerns about altered behavior or other signs of depersonalization. Carelessness in preparations, lessening of commitment, increasing lateness or absence from service or meetings, and expressions of frustrations during the welcoming moments are a few of the clear indications that burnout has begun to smolder.

Short, regular, but spiritually strong meetings can also aid in avoiding a trend of depersonalization among your team. These meetings can include intermittent training and orientation for new members, but they might also include invited guests who speak on new subject matter that connects with the ministry. Possible guest speakers would be a psychologist or sociologist who addresses matters of mental state or body language; a homemaker or hotelier who can talk about the art of hospitality; or a leader from another church with a flourishing greeter ministry. Do not hesitate to bring any professional person into your meetings to be quizzed by your teammates as well as to teach during an appropriate and timely workshop. Do not take for granted that all believers know how to greet or have developed the capacities needed and necessary for greeting worshipers.

Technology. In small churches with limited resources or in large churches with cathedral-like space, technology can be a challenge. Since team leaders need to be able to communicate while on duty, ensuring appropriate coverage and maintenance of entryways, most greeter ministries utilize the fairly basic technology of handheld two-way radios, more commonly known as walkie-talkies. Such devices are moderately priced, and the cost outlay proves to be a worthy investment in support of quality service. The reward will be a team that feels connected with one another throughout the building rather than feeling disconnected or isolated from those stationed in other entryways.

This kind of technology can also be used to facilitate communication and coordination of multiple ministries. Individuals who serve as greeters, ushers, parking-lot attendants, security guards, and deacons often find it valuable to be in communication—not just within their own ministry but also with others serving in various capacities. All of this is relative to the size of your congregation and facility, of course, but communication technology is usually a must in order to appropriately accommodate your worshipers.

Remembering names. Worshipers appreciate a greeter who welcomes them by name each Sunday. Not everyone has a gift for matching faces with names—and recalling that match after a week or a month of time. Particularly as we age, memory for names and faces may become a challenge. No matter how much of a challenge this is for you, make an attempt to the best of your ability. The effort is always appreciated.

Don't be anxious or discouraged if this is a struggle for you or for your team as a whole, but consider offering a workshop on creative ways to remember names and faces. Make it an element of your enrichment program. Get creative with mnemonic devices. If your church has a pictorial directory, get an extra copy or two and cut it up. Use the photo and name combinations in team games of matching or flashcards. Or circulate the names and faces among the team members, each week or month assigning specific church members to each greeter as subjects of intercessory prayer. It's amazing how regular prayer for a stranger will fix that person's identity in your memory. It will be fun learning the myriad ways of committing things and people to memory.

Attendance. As with any volunteer ministry, greeters are susceptible to tardiness and absenteeism. Deal with both challenges openly and honestly from the beginning. Approach the potential problem from a covenantal perspective, encouraging each team member to covenant with one another not to leave other greeters stranded without sufficient staff in place. This includes taking the role seriously enough to be at church and in place on time. Find ways to personally encourage and strengthen the resolve of each member for the greater well-being of the team.

Many will not see this role and level of service as being spiritual. They will need to be taught that what they offer to worshipers each Sunday morning is far more than a smile and handshake but ultimately an expression of the spirit of Christ emanating from within. The degree to which they will see their role as spiritual is the degree to which they will be taught it is biblical.

Crowd control. This is a particular challenge for larger congregations and for churches with more than one service on a Sunday morning. It will also present more of a problem for the novice on your team. Not being sensitive to or knowledgeable about the measurements of the entryways relative to arrival of worshipers, greeters may need to be steeped in a bit of crowd control. Gently handled, they can help to steer worshipers in one direction or another should the narthex or entryway become a bit too crowded.

Should this be a need, it presents an excellent opportunity to coordinate with the ushers relative to which doors the earlier service will depart from and, therefore, which doors are available for arriving worshipers. Roped-off areas might be necessary if large crowds tend to gather at entryways before worshipers in the earlier service depart. All preparation for this should be made ahead of time! I cannot stress the importance of this enough. You must anticipate, not wait until a crowd forms and then respond. Each greeter should know how to direct arriving worshipers for a successive service to keep chaos and confusion at a minimum. Again, this requires the best coordination of ministry heads, ushers, team leaders, and greeters for smooth transitions. Such routines must be practiced to facilitate the ease of carrying out such tasks.

While people are in line or grouped and waiting for the earlier service to conclude, use this valuable time to go down the line with several key reminders:

> Please remember to turn off all cell phones.
> Here's a bulletin so that when the doors open you can go right in.
> Our nursery is available for all babies and children (stating ages accepted).
> Children's church for those aged _____ to _____ meets in room _____ (and mention whatever other age-appropriate ministries you might have on Sunday mornings).
> Our café/dining room is open if you would like to wait more comfortably there.

Inability to worship. Perhaps the most basic challenge associated with the work of the greeter is one that is common to any service ministry. Many people find it difficult to worship when they are on duty. Subsequently, many greeters leave the building almost as soon as they leave their post. Strongly discourage this as unacceptable behavior—and present a biblical argument for cultivating a spirit of worship and fellowship, even (and especially) when serving as a gatekeeper. Worship and service should be commingled, not separated. We do not choose to worship one Sunday and serve on a different Sunday and the two seldom if ever meet. Talk as a team and help one another find personal ways of making the human-divine connection, even while maintaining your positions during the worship experience. To bifurcate the two is not a healthy spirituality. Doing God's work God's way *is* an act of worship.

No challenge is too small to overlook, and no challenge is too great that it cannot be overcome. Do not let the challenges overwhelm you. As a leader in this ministry, know your church. Know your people. Know the Scriptures that give birth to such a ministry. Know and develop your own giftedness in the area of hospitality. Drench your team in prayer before going to your various posts. By that I mean offer more than just a sentence or two of prayer; don't appoint one person to lead in prayer. Depending upon the size of your team, have several members—if not all—of your team participate. Separate into smaller groups if necessary to engage in this season of prayer in preparation for your greeter service. With prayer and preparation, I am confident that no challenge will go unmet.

CHAPTER 8

Spiritual Development of the Greeter

To greet arriving worshipers is to seek to enhance and elevate the level of spiritual expectancy in worship. Its task is to awaken in the arriving worshiper an increased awareness of where he or she is (in the house of God) and the reason for being there (to be blessed by the presence and power of God). Whereas the usher provides the practical needs of a bulletin and a pew, the greeters' best tools are breath through which they verbalize acceptance and welcome and an affirming handshake or embrace. While the usher provides the place and space wherein the worshiper will sit, it is the greeter who conditions the quality and openness to the Spirit as worshipers take their seats.

Many denominations have used the term "lay ministry" over the years, but most parishioners still see themselves as workers without the ministry tag attached to their service. It is difficult to develop greeters spiritually without their being able to see themselves as serving the cause of Christ through their work in his kingdom. This point is not merely a matter of semantics. Nor is it an attempt to elevate the significance of the greeters' role. If greeting does not emanate from the depth of a healthy, hospitality-oriented, caring spirit, then the quality of greeting of your worshipers will not occur. Without a caring spirit, the role then becomes perfunctory; a mere caricature of what it means to be warmly and genuinely welcomed. The activity becomes an act, and the service remains superficial.

The work of the greeter is not limited to a well-dressed or uniformed member positioned near a church entrance with an outstretched, gloved hand and a pasted-on smile. Such an image is a vain and superficial caricature of a real greeter! Such an image values style over substance. A true greeter creates an atmosphere of genuine spiritual warmth and human acceptance of those entering into the house of the Lord. For this reason, practical training and functional orientation are not sufficient preparation for your team of greeters. To these pragmatic elements, you must be sure to add ongoing spiritual development for all members of the team. When taken seriously, such spiritual development will transform ordinary tasks into an extension of the evangelistic efforts of your congregation.

Use Scripture in your meetings and workshops, or share sessions to help overcome judgmental attitudes, being shy, being too sensitive to people's responses, or lacking sensitivity. Plan Bible studies to develop a curriculum around the personality needs of greeters. You will realize that the rightness of the greeter's role to welcome worshipers and greet them with grace and care is not a twenty-first-century idea but is as old as Abraham and beyond.

It is important to trace the lineage of this task back to Scripture and know not only the tradition of your particular denomination, congregation, or culture. Your membership might go back fifty years; your congregational history might even be well over one hundred years; your denomination could go back as far as the Protestant Reformation—the 1600s. Your historical-cultural traditions are by now even imbedded in your DNA. But none of them go back far enough to provide you, as door-keepers, with the depth of comprehension of what God would have you doing in the church where you serve. Biblical notation and confirmation are important pieces of information to provide the depth of understanding anyone needs to modulate or modify one's behavior in the church today.

As officers and team leaders, you are encouraged to be as serious about the spiritual development as you might be about dress, presentation, and safety.

Start with your monthly meetings. This is where you set the tone and raise the expectation of how spiritual growth will be nurtured and sustained. This is where you make it important so that it can flow throughout the rest of your organization's service to the church. Remind people that you are not simply interested in grinners but greeters! You are looking for prospective greeters who want to be steeped in the best biblical tradition of welcoming people into a building and filled with the deeper purpose of welcoming worshipers into the presence of God.

Balance your meeting with spiritual nurture and biblical orientation on the subject of hospitality. Talk about its need and relevance in the church today.

Ask the pastor if greeters can take charge of Bible study for a week or even do a four-week series that may utilize the biblical basis and texts from this book. You accomplish three things with this: you help to educate the congregation; you strengthen the learning of your greeters as they prepare to present; and you underscore the level of serious commitment that is needed in the ministry of greeting.

Compose a spiritual check-up motto to say to one another when on duty. Here are a few possibilities:

> "Check your spirit!"
> "Is my spirit showing?"
> "Mirror, mirror on the wall, let my spirit show most of all!"
> "Grace shows on my face!"
> "Spirit's leading the way"!
> "Grace is in place!"
> "We're Spirit-ready!"

Encourage private spiritual devotions: at home, before service, and on duty.

Feed your greeters with a different Bible verse each month that they learn to recite silently while on duty that will inspire, focus, and encourage them.

Don't discount your need for worship. What you have given up in order to serve would best be balanced with another Sunday or weekday worship service.

Spiritual Nourishment: Lessons from Ezra, Mary and Martha
The Old Testament book of Ezra may not be the first place we go to for our chosen spiritual nourishment. Yet, I chose this book of the Bible because the account in Ezra, chapters 7 and 8 sets out some principles that we can apply to the ministry of greeting.

Ezra, a scribe (one who copied and studied the Word of God) and teacher, led his people's spiritual growth and efforts to re-build the temple in one of the most difficult times of his nation's history. After returning from exile in Babylon, Ezra wasn't seeking prominence, but he stepped into a place of leadership after finding that not one Levite (God's commissioned priests) had come to Jerusalem with this wave of exiles. Since God's temple had no ministers, Ezra sent messengers to Iddo, the leader of the Levites, to request priests for the temple at Jerusalem. In his passion to lead God's people, Ezra acknowledged no fewer than five times that "the gracious hand of the Lord my God was on me" (NLT).

From these facts we can learn three things. First, God uses whom God chooses. And although Ezra was a member of a priestly family, you don't need to be a priest to do priestly things; you function in a priestly role any time you are leading God's people. Next, Ezra's concern for the house of the Lord and for his people shines through in his request that Iddo send priests to serve the Lord in the temple. In a similar way, greeters can share and show that concern. Finally, like Ezra, greeters can feel encouraged because "the gracious hand of the LORD my God [is] on me" (Ezra 7:28 NLT). Keeping these things in mind, you are ready for leadership. Greater leadership skill will come in the doing.

The pivotal reason I chose the book of Ezra as spiritual nour-ishment for greeters is found in Ezra 8:28-29 (NKJV). In those verses, Ezra spoke to twelve of the priests: "And I said to them, 'You are holy to the LORD; the articles are holy also; and the silver and the gold are a freewill offering to the LORD God of your fathers. Watch and keep them until you weigh them before the leaders of the priests and the Levites and heads of the fathers' houses of Israel in Jerusalem, in the chambers of the house of the LORD.'" Those who had been selected to minister in the temple were highly praised and valued as being "holy unto the Lord." They were instruments in God's hands to become blessings to the people of God. So it is with greeters. You are instruments in the hands of God to become blessings to the people of God.

Ezra 8:36 goes on to say, "and they further supported the people and house of God." Despite the mentioning of the "24 tons of silver, 7,500 pounds of silver utensils, 7,500 pounds of gold, [and] 20 gold bowls," Ezra seemed to have valued those who served the temple over the treasure *of* the temple. Occasionally in church we tend to value things over people. The communion table is at least by tradition and dedication "holy unto the Lord," and people wince if they see someone putting something on it that doesn't belong there. However, Ezra 8:35-36 suggest a sense of the sacred, not just with objects used in worship but also those who handle those sacred objects in worship. Like the silver and gold items the exiles brought with them from Babylon to help furnish the temple, you as greeters are instruments in God's hands to use in the building up not necessarily of a church edifice but of the lives of people.

Team leaders cannot go too far in helping your greeters deepen their affection for God's people. The world has ingrained in us every way to think of others as less than ourselves: by age, race, education, gender, possessions, speech, what we drive, abilities, or where we live. These differences so often elicit automatic responses when we encounter a person that we hardly give a thought as to how we have sized up him or her. The world has ingrained in us that our differences are the only qualities that define us or that count. Well, not in God's house…not with God's people. That's the power of Ezra's saga: no matter how much the Jews had sinned and failed to keep God's law, Ezra stood in the gap for them, called them back to God, and felt no need to lapse into a judgmental attitude about them.

That is the idea to be held dear as you serve in the ministry of greeting: regardless of how holy certain items are in the church, God's people are holier. God has raised up the people over and above the things in the temple or sanctuary—knowing all the time how holy those things were. Always recall: Christ did not die for things. He died for people…you, and the people you welcome on Sundays. Allow this thought to inform, infuse, and inspire your quality of greeting.

A good New Testament Bible study for your team might focus on the story of the biblical Mary and Martha—how one was in the kitchen and the other was at the feet of Jesus. It is suggested by William J. Carter in *Team Spirituality* that both "Martha's hard work and Mary's spiritual attentiveness" are to be more seriously considered because "one without the other is powerless…bringing [that understanding] to a mature spirituality and full effectiveness."[1]

If your understanding of hospitality is punch and cookies, then your journey into the real ministry of hospitality is about to begin. If your understanding of hospitality is primarily food-oriented, then you have missed the myriad moments of biblical hospitality, which is foundational to ministry in the Old and New Testaments. Although food was and is often an essential element of hospitality, it is not the central focus of hospitality.

Most of my church life, the church has reveled in lauding Mary while holding Martha in disdain, as though she just did not get it! Let's be clear: houses must be cleaned and guests must be prepared for to some degree. Prayers, meditation, and study of the Word must be done as well. I believe that over the years the church has tended to polarize what Jesus sought to harmonize. Jesus loved being in the home of Mary, Martha, and Lazarus; each was dear to him as a friend. At their house in Bethany, Jesus was a frequent beneficiary of their gracious hospitality. He never sought to pit Mary against Martha as he declared that "Mary had chosen the best part" because she sat attentively at his feet for spiritual instruction while Martha labored vigorously in the kitchen.

The words of Jesus are more suggestive of getting priorities straight than of using "prayer and meditation" as ways to opt out of one's responsibilities. It is a practical example of his earlier instruction, "Seek the Kingdom of God above all else, and live righteously, and he will give you everything you need" (Matthew 6:33 NLT). It's not prayer versus practical preparation. Evidently Jesus enjoyed being hosted, but he never wanted anyone to lose sight of his real value: his presence. Frying chicken and setting the table for dinner could wait a bit, because filling our stomachs while leaving our spirits empty is not how he wants us to live. Neither is it the way to live successfully: "the best part" must come first; then the Lord will balance, order, strengthen, focus, and prioritize our lives as he did for Martha. He will also diminish our stress.

Cultural Expressions of Hospitality

Not only have I searched through Scriptures to offer some appropriate biblical texts for this book, but also I have researched various cultures concerning their ways of greeting. Having traveled to forty-two different countries—some as many as fifteen to twenty times—I've long been intrigued about the ways various cultures have of greeting guests. These diverse ways of life have much to teach us as we consider the role and tasks and spiritual condition of those choosing to serve on greeter teams.

The core of any culture is formed by the values it chooses to express. And, throughout every culture some expression of hospitality and a sense of welcoming the traveler or stranger in their midst is evident. Making my plans to travel to the isle of Patmos in Greece, I could not book a hotel on that island, and there were plenty. Concerned, I called the local Greek Orthodox church to speak with the pastor, who told me not to worry. He explained the custom of that culture: local citizens met every boat (the only means of arrival and departure) and offered perfect strangers a place to stay, usually at an unadvertised bed and breakfast. So, therefore, I should not worry, because there would *always* be a place to stay!

True to his word, upon my arrival a man in a pickup truck pulled up to me and inquired about my hotel arrangements. I did something I would never do in any other place and space: I got into the car with a man I did not know to ride to an undisclosed location to sleep in a place I had never seen or heard of. But on the word of that pastor back in the States, I trusted the culture to provide hospitality in ways people had been doing for a few thousand years. It worked. I could not have had a lovelier place: one with beautiful tropical flowers on my balcony overlooking the town and the Mediterranean Sea. This cultural expression of hospitality is more vivid in my mind nearly ten years later than some of the historic sites that graced my eyes.

While most cultures have a simple word or two of greeting, others have specific ways of kissing cheeks. But there are some with unique ways of making people welcome. In Belize, people press their fists together, a gesture that has a parallel in modern American culture as a popular way of saluting folk or ac-knowledging agreement—called "the fist bump." In Japan, peo-ple bow from the waist, while in New Zealand, the Maori people press their noses together to greet one another. In Kenya, the word *Jambo* is declared enthusiastically and is usually fol-lowed by a hug or handshake. In Hawaii, a rope of fragrant flowers, called a lei, is draped around your neck while natives dance you from ship to shore or from airport to taxi.[2]

A traditional greeting in India is, to me, the most unique and closest to our sense of valuing those we encounter. On encoun-tering someone or entering a home, palms are placed together in a prayerful style with fingers pointed heavenward. The position of the hands, which are centered in front, shifts from above one's heart to lower than one's heart depending upon whether an adult or child is being greeted. If one is greeting a child, the hands are lower than one's own heart, but if one is greeting a person of honor (e.g., an elderly person, parents), then hands are above the heart signifying respect for them. But what they say to all is *Namaste*—"I recognize the god in you."

Christians do not believe that persons themselves are gods or God, but they do honor the supreme Being in whose image human beings are made. Oh, if within Christianity and at the door of the sanctuary, we too could have that quality of reverence for all who enter! It seems to me that this quality of respect is significant in the theology that supports the work of the greeter. In our ministry, we must constantly remind ourselves of how valuable each person is who chooses to enter our church. Each one carries within him or herself the image of God—and the presence of God's own Spirit. What a wonderful perspective to have on each human being. Valuing our fellow worshipers in such ways shapes a more spiritual context within which we live our lives and carry on our ministry.

I've been told that "patience, attentiveness and sensitivity are not common…traits, but they can help in cultures different from our own."[3] This is true because each and every culture has at its core a quality and quantity of hospitality, and the Christian church should have no less as it welcomes people to worship.

Why don't you consider surprising your parishioners by using multicultural expressions of welcome? You need not limit your greeting to just a smile and handshake, although creative alternatives should be introduced only after you have engaged in the spiritual development of studying the other culture and understanding the significance and/or theology behind a particular mode of greeting. You might try the fist bump. Or you could add background music to your greeting moments, which could also signal a deeper reverence or heightened joy as people prepare to enter the sanctuary. Music often accompanies various cultural greetings.

Often some form of dance also is part of a given culture's greeting. So, you might consider having dancers or singers form two rows, creating a path for the guests to walk down. You might consider tapping the talents of your church's dance troupe to help in welcoming, perhaps on a Sunday of a major church celebration. In great joy, dancers have also touched the arm of arriving guests in a gentle ushering mode while leading them toward the entryway.

Putting It into Practice: Reflections

Most of this book has been proactive and instructive, seeking to provide you with credible tools with which you can build and sustain your greeters' ministry. You will find that along with your effort to build a ministry of greeting and to construct a viable service organization in your church, you will need to be just as diligent at getting the kinks out. I have found that the following hindrances often work to undermine the quality of ministry: poor listening, lack of forgiveness, reliance on stereotypes, and lack of appreciation for others' efforts. These, along with a minimalist perspective on hospitality (i.e., that it is usually food-connected) can hinder growth in your greeters and will also hinder a more meaningful and comprehensive view of greeting in the house of the Lord. To counteract these perspectives, the following paragraphs will ask your team members to reflect on their ministry and make suggestions for changes.

Listening

In *Hearing Beyond the Words,* Emma Justes equates true hospitality with being able to listen to another person. She says, "Because of the centrality of receiving in listening, listening can be understood as an act of hospitality. Listening, like hospitality, not only involves receiving another person, but includes being welcoming and open to the speaker who is in our presence."[4]

She follows this with a declaration that the "ability to listen is rooted in the person or character of the listener, as is hospitality."[5] "From the beginning of the story of the people of Israel," she declares, "hospitality is a core value. Their experiences of being strangers in foreign lands, being slaves in Egypt, and wandering in the desert gave the people a clear sense of the value of hospitality. Being hospitable became a sign of being faithful."[6]

Whether taking orders at a fast-food drive-through or giving information over the phone, the reality is that we are often poor listeners. It has little to do with our ears and everything to do with our ability to more adequately attend to the other person. Good listening skills will increase our ability to focus better on the person and shut out distractions within and around us.

For reflection and discussion: Think of a recent conversation with a member or visitor to your church. What happened during that conversation? Were there verbal cues that you might have missed? What were they? What distractions influenced the course of the conversation? How might you have focused only on the person? What could you have said or done differently?

The Spirit of Grace

Experiencing the grace of God in our lives enlarges our capacity for kindness and graciousness. Within your team, frequently celebrate someone's experience of God's grace (not necessarily connected with the duty of greeting). Then watch as this experience of grace begins to season the behavior of the team in greater kindness and graciousness. Few experiences of grace transform us as God's forgiveness when we know we have failed or disobeyed him! Because of God's powerful forgiveness in our lives, our hearts are filled with kindness and graciousness toward others.

The power of spiritual preparedness is reckoned with by author and New Testament scholar Richard Longenecker in *Into God's Presence,* in which he declares:

> A wrong attitude to prayer is also present when people are not willing to forgive others, even as they pray that God will extend forgiveness to them (Mark 11:25). The rationale for this statement is expressed most clearly in the parable of the unforgiving servant of Matthew 18:21-35. Here Jesus brings out the enormity of the action of a servant who was forgiven his own enormous debt, which he was unable to pay, but who endeavors to exact the full amount of a comparatively trivial debt from another servant, who is equally unable to pay. The

force of the parable renders argument superfluous. God will not forgive those whose lives are not changed by the grace that they experience.[7]

For reflection and discussion: How would you respond to the preceding quote? Suppose that a petty grievance festers between two members of the greeters' team. Describe what some of the resulting behaviors might be. How might this affect the greeters' ministry? the congregation? How might the two people resolve their disagreement? What might be your role, as a fellow greeter, to help resolve the disagreement? What Scripture passages apply?

Due Diligence

Too much of life is lived with the body in one place and the mind or the desire of the heart someplace entirely different. Seek to bring all of you into the greeting moment. Such encounters are brief, yet they can have a lengthy and even eternal, impact if accomplished or offered in the right way and with the right spirit. Put out of your mind the difficulties you may have encountered prior to your arrival at the church or your concerns about what you are planning to have for dinner. Nothing on earth is more important than your ability to appropriately, enthusiastically, and genuinely greet incoming worshipers. Acts 15:8 tells us, "God…knows the heart." You are partnering with God in helping to make his house "a house of prayer for all people" as you welcome and engage them for that purpose.

For reflection and discussion: To what distractions are you prone? How might you better prepare for the task of greeting?

How might you need to rearrange your priorities or your time? As a group, brainstorm to create a list of Scripture passages that will help you to focus on the sanctuary as a house of prayer. Choose one passage to meditate on this week as you prepare for your service as a greeter.

Boundaries

While welcoming new ministry trends into your church, even establishing or strengthening a greeters' ministry, you're also seeking to break down boundaries that are socially established in the secular world but should not exist among believers. Greeters accept "whosoever" comes through that door. Some may need help, some may need sympathy, some may need counseling, all could use a smile...all of which serves to reduce or render ineffective the boundaries that prevent believers from readily accepting others and from ultimately becoming one, as Jesus prayed in John 17. It is not that we have to be the same. It is that we have to accept one another's differences and then shape those differences into commonalities in the faith. Lose who you are and become what Christ has called you to be as you welcome those who are coming to seek, honor, and worship him.

For reflection and discussion: What assumptions have you made recently about a visitor or a member of your congregation? Why did you make those assumptions? What can you do to change your attitudes? How can you manifest that change in the way you greet people? How can your fellow greeters help you and hold you accountable?

Gifts, Ribbons, Winners!

Do you like to receive gifts unexpectedly? Consider having a token gift, such as a Scripture card or ribbon, a couple of times a year. I remember one of the neighborly gestures a friend of mine vividly recalls because of its impact on her. I knew she was a home economist and was used to awarding blue ribbons to winners. So after a very kind act on her part—and to show my appreciation—I went to the door of her house through which she most often enters and tied a beautiful blue ribbon on the doorknob. Without words, it declared what a winner—and first-class friend—she was. A tiny gesture, but a lasting impact that she still recalls. Some of your worshipers may not know or recall "why a blue ribbon," but if you write the word "winner" on it, there is no doubt that it will brighten their day, and they will never forget the church that declared them a winner!

For reflection and discussion: How can you show appreciation for your fellow greeters? church members? visitors? As a group, brainstorm ideas, choose the best ones, and plan when and how you'll express your appreciation. As part of your planning, study relevant Scripture passages about building up one another.

In *Life Principles for Worship from the Tabernacle,* author and pastor Wayne Barber writes:

> Every morning when they awoke, the landscape might be different, but as they looked from their tent, the Tabernacle would be sitting in the same position and facing the same direction. They were learning to follow

God *moment by moment,* and they were learning to keep Him at the very center of their lives—see Numbers 2:1-16.[8] ...Although the Tabernacle moved often during its nearly 500 years of use, one thing remained constant. It was always at the very center of the camp and the nation.[9]

Greeters, your degree of readiness is measured spiritually by whether you have allowed God to take ownership of his place at the center of your lives. He can be in your walk or in your talk, even in your heart and soul, but his desire is to be at the core of your being—in your spirit—powerfully emanating from the center of your life.

How can you measure whether you are ready to serve? Your willingness to serve is the first level of readiness. You are encouraged to move to the greater depth or greatest possible height of readiness to worship by growing in your biblical understanding of what it means to worship God. Your worship readiness on Sundays is a sure outgrowth of your private, individual devotions all during the week.

Members and visitors come to church because they want to find God there, enter his presence, and worship. What better place is there to greet God's people as they make their way to worship him? How better to prepare them to encounter God than by reflecting the warmth and care of God? I pray that your ministry of greeting shall have this quality and this depth of offering to your congregation!

APPENDIX

Training Module for Greeters' Ministry

This module will provide you with some insights relative to structuring your group and essential training areas that will strengthen your team as you endeavor to offer sincere hospitality as a natural expression of your faith.

A rigorous training cycle should be offered at the beginning of a greeters' ministry. Continuing training, workshops, and orientations in areas supportive of excellence in hospitality and greeting are required. Motives should be examined. Levels of commitment to greeting and passion for hospitality are essential to discern. Remember that training is not a single event but an ongoing process in order to have the quality of the team that you desire and your church deserves.

Recruitment

Endeavor not to accept "whosoever will." Instead, set some standards. Look for a level of spiritual maturity. Though this is not a place for babes in Christ, it could be a wonderful area of service for members who have manifested growth and experience in the church. Look for those who show natural warmth toward others. Search out those who know that ministry is not about them but about others.

Don't recruit only your proven leaders. Include those you discern have some wonderful potential in this area, thereby not making the responsibility too heavy on a few people. Forget the old adage, "If you want something done, find a busy person." That leads to overload, overuse, and even a level of abuse of church leaders, while many who might want to share in this ministry are left in the pews. Do your normal advertising, but also approach people personally whom you might have noticed could fulfill most of your expectations around greeting worshipers.

You know that most "liabilities" in your recruits can be dealt with through the training they will receive. Your efforts also should be to develop your team and bring some balanced greeting behaviors that you cannot take for granted that people know. Such training will contribute to the overall hospitality of your congregation that many members will learn only through such an opportunity. Anyone with appropriate training can improve and even conquer some personality traits that could potentially undermine effectiveness as a greeter. Make certain that the training you offer is required, and not optional. This will ensure that your full team will have the same skills and awareness relative to offering hospitable greetings to entering worshipers.

Scheduling / Rotation / Roster

Optimally, you should have a bench of at least five people deep for each and every post you discern is needed to adequately greet parishioners. I say this to suggest that each person would serve only once or twice a month. Therefore, according to your rotational requirements you would need another person for the other

Sundays plus a roster of substitutes. Those are persons who do not want to make a full commitment but would help out in a pinch. That would give you the luxury of having one person serve only one week a month plus a substitute or on-call person in case of emergencies or planned absences. Depending upon the size of your congregation, if you need only five greeters to handle your Sunday crowd, then your rotational grid would have fifteen other team members if they are to serve one Sunday each month and a total of ten if they are serving two Sundays each month. You can also give part of your cadre of greeters a month off during the summer (half in July and half in August) because attendance is normally somewhat less during the summer months.

Very large congregations have as many as three hundred active greeters. Simply discern how many are needed for one service on one Sunday; then calculate how many you need for two or three services on each Sunday, and schedule your greeters in rotation depending whether they are serving once or twice a month. Most often the teams would serve multiple services on their given Sunday; however, this can also be broken down into service rotation for a specific service on a specific Sunday.

Prepare job descriptions for each position in the greeters' ministry. Here is a suggested list.

Team leader: assumes the basic responsibility for all greeters, including recruitment, training, development, and coordination with other church leaders (e.g., pastor, trustees, deacons, ushers, medics, etc.).

Co-team leader: assists in the above-mentioned duties. You should have as many of these as you have separate teams for different entrances of the church. Co-team leaders are ones who would be capable of assuming the team leader position should it become vacant.

Scheduler: takes responsibility for gathering all contact information and service rotation. Individual greeters should be made responsible for securing a greeter to substitute for them if and when they cannot fulfill their assigned duty.

Development coordinator: helps in the practical and spiritual development of all team members and makes certain that they have undergone the proper (available) training.

Add any other officer to the team as your specific circumstances might need.

Many of your members might have demonstrated being gifted in the area of hospitality and in the abilities of welcoming people. Select wisely. Some who may have been trained in CPR or other emergency care techniques should be especially recruited to ensure that at least one or two serves on a greeters' team each Sunday.

Balance

It is essential that there is balance on your team and that each demographic area is represented: male, female, young, mature. Don't recruit only individuals; also consider families who would serve as greeters on the same Sunday. Children from eight to eighteen, with appropriate training and supervision, can serve with other family members. This is one easy yet critical area where ministry can successfully be intergenerational.

Bring balance to your team also by being determined to

recruit more men into your group. Men often need to be invited directly. Express that need to individual men, and they will respond appropriately. Men are needed not just for their warmth and smiles but also for their brawn and the sense of security they may bring into any situation, even greeting. You need them to help some of the elderly. You need them to especially—and playfully—welcome some of the children. You need them to help a woman carrying a baby and holding onto a child or two while holding other appropriate items as well.

It may be that a person who has had traumatic experiences would feel uneasy being greeted by a man. If a worshiper feels in any way intimidated or inappropriately greeted by a male greeter, then that should be reported immediately and dealt with accordingly. However, women and youth will also be serving, so a worshiper has the option of walking towards them, if that is what he or she prefers. Remember that five, or twenty, or fifty or more greeters are strewn throughout the narthex. Also, the moment of greeting is comparatively brief, and there should not be places of seclusion where untoward behaviors could happen. We still need to recruit men and not leave greeting only to just women and youth.

The ultimate balance is to recruit families. Plan this appeal. Launch a special appeal to offer them the opportunity—one of the few in the life of the church—to serve together as a family. Plan the ideal position(s) where families could best serve so that they will be pleased with their station. It may be near the nursery or the church entrance closest to children's church. However, families are not necessarily limited to such specific church entrances, because other families enter through all doors and then find their way to their chosen sites once they are inside.

Ensure that applicants know this is a spiritual development opportunity and not a first-rung task in the church. Reassure them with your plans to mold together a team of greeters fully prepared to welcome those who are coming to worship the Lord. Let them know that the quality of training that you will provide will guarantee them that quality of growth in their lives and in the lives of those they warmly welcome.

It's easy to select people who seem normally outgoing, but they are not the only ones you want on your team. People who seem personable and outgoing can often be those who might focus more on themselves than on the entering worshipers. Look for balance and mix your options.

Consider some of the many tests that are now available to help you and your volunteers discern their spiritual giftedness. Although this is not essential, some churches now offer all of their leaders the opportunity to be tested in this manner. Two such tests are Church Volunteer Central and D.I.S.C. "Multiplying ministry from me to we and guiding people into their gift-based ministry is critical to recruiting, motivating, and retaining volunteers," declares Church Volunteer Central. D.I.S.C. stands for "Dominance," which measures behaviors "relating to control, power and assertiveness;" "Influence," which relates "to social situations and communication;" "Steadiness," which relates to "patience, persistence, and thoughtfulness; and "Conscientiousness," which measures one's ability "to structure and organize." Contact and further descriptive information about both tests can easily be found on the Internet.

There are also some tests that compare contemporary church members with biblical characters of similar personality types and offer fun and interesting conversations for those being tested. Review these tests carefully, because some can be a bit expensive. However, don't be fooled into thinking that cheaper is better, since you may not obtain the depth of discovery needed in the person(s) being tested. The results are worth the investment as they support the quality of ministry you envision.

The Act of Greeting
Some people believe that the greeter should introduce himself or herself. This makes the moment cumbersome and shapes the encounter around the greeter and the congregation rather than around the presence and needs of the arriving worshiper. Remember, this act of greeting is not to present the church or the greeter to the greeted; rather, it is to make the arriving worshiper feel warmly welcomed in the church, safe, and accepted in its midst.

Knowing What to Say
Being thrust into a crowd of people entering the church might leave you a bit tongue-tied initially, but if you stay tuned in to their possible needs you will do more than smile and will think of more to say than "Welcome!" Notice their demeanor—rushed, leisurely, harried, slightly disheveled, bringing children. Then notice their affect: whether they look jubilant or sad,

worried or emotionless. Any and all of these signs can help you know how to greet people individually rather than having one word for everyone who comes through the door. Here are some questions that will prompt your response to their approach.

- What are they carrying?
- Who are they with?
- How fast are they walking?
- Where are they looking (down, around, or straight ahead)? "Down" might suggest deep thought; "around" could suggest a security consciousness, some confusion about direction of the sanctuary (or other needs), or curiosity about being in a new church while "straight ahead" suggests that they are focused and generally know where they are going.
- What kind of facial expression do they have? Serious? Jovial? Angry? Inquisitive? Tuning in to who they are in the moment can prompt concern in the greeter and appropriate inquiry rather than just the cookie-cutter greeting "Welcome!" You have the advantage of watching them in their approach long before they realize you are watching. Make mental notes about the change in their demeanor or facial expression as they draw closer to your position.

Whether you are in a grocery store or in an upscale department store, the way to capture, amaze, and truly be inviting in your efforts to welcome and greet is to give more than the person expects. That's how you clearly demonstrate your desire to have them return. Here are some possibilities.

Joy: "Glad you're here today!" Examine your personal feelings. Are you exemplifying the attitude of the father to the returning son or the attitude of the elder brother? Do you really want new people in your church? Then that ebullience should manifest in your joyous expression(s) toward the incoming worshiper.

Humor: "Slow down! You're in time!" If you see people hurrying, a little humor will bring relaxation. You can then be helpful, providing directions if needed or necessary.

Helpful: "Your arms are full! May I help you?" (You see a mother with a baby, baby stuff, plus a child in tow.) This is one of the few reasons for leaving your post; however, a quick return is expected. Don't wait for someone to ask for help. Offer it!

Concern: "Are you all right?" You will not have a clue as to what might have just happened to this worshiper. A call, a thought, a parking-lot experience with another worshiper...on and on! However, raise the concern and demonstrate your care. The person may need to be taken aside for a moment, or a minister or deacon may need to be called. Be attentive, and be flexible.

Send off: "Enjoy the worship!" Once all is well, refocus people with this word of encouragement because at least temporarily they would have been focused on other things.

Recognition: "Great to see you back again!" (Be certain to whom you are saying that!) Folk will know you are insincere or have made a big mistake if you say this to them and they have never worshiped at your church before. Be careful with your familiarity. Attempt to become more and more familiar with your members but not artificially so.

Information: "It's _____ today, and we're glad you're here!" The arriving worshipers might not remember that "today is the pastor's anniversary" or some other celebrated day. Celebrate it with them via your declarative welcome. It's at once a reminder as well as an invitation to join in the celebration.

Orientation: "Welcome!" This, plus an extended hand, is the minimal of what can be said upon the arrival of your worshipers. However, try to vary your quality of welcoming statements when possible.

Stance and Attire

The most welcoming stance is to stand comfortably straight with hands outstretched partially in front of you as though you are preparing to hug someone. It is easy from that posture to hug if a person's demeanor suggests such—particularly children—or to switch to a handshake or pat on the shoulder. Make the connection with the handshake, an embrace, or a pat on the arm, shoulder, or back.

Make certain that you are in comfortable shoes. It is important that you not wear perfume or cologne out of consideration of the many allergies that people have. Be careful and intentional about your personal hygiene. And by all means, have on the agreed-upon attire or sash or badge so that you can easily be identified as an official greeter.

The Greeter's Practical and Spiritual Preparation

Your task as a greeter is first of all spiritual and then practical. Mouthing welcoming words with a friendly facial expression is obvious, but learn to smile with your eyes and not just with your mouth. To smile with your eyes is spiritual. To smile with your eyes necessitates looking into a person's face…into his or her eyes…connecting…communicating your joy in that person's presence. Your ability to do that easily moves you well beyond just doing the task of greeting and into the essence of the role of greeter.

You, too, have gone through a lot to be ready to serve—from opening your eyes that morning to mounting your post. You have already been moving toward your post for several hours and have possibly focused only on the practical things you needed to get done on Sunday morning before arriving at church. Your spiritual preparation is paramount so that you will be freshly renewed to focus on the stranger in your midst.

Ongoing Training and Spiritual Development

All of these considerations are paramount to launch your greeters' ministry; however, these topics also present possibilities for ongoing training in addition to the need for spiritual nurture and development. It would be great and grand to invite a psychologist and a sociologist to educate team members about personality needs in this important ministry as a way to orient and sensitize your greeters to those they are welcoming. They can learn some body language as well as being oriented to certain facial expressions. It could be quite helpful.

Select someone who is gifted in the area of hospitality and sees it as ministry. It has been my experience that Roman Catholics have done the most work in this area, and many nuns serve where they are—such as retreat centers—because they are gifted in the areas of spirituality and hospitality. One example is Sister Cathy, who has been given the ministry of hospitality and oversees Shalom House, to which every denominational group in the region flocks because of the quality of care. There is clear balance between latitude allowed to those on retreat and guidelines relative to behaviors that are not allowed. She manages beautifully to put people at ease so that they are free to focus on the purposes for which they have come. By contrast, most Protestant congregations tend to think of chicken and green beans when the word "hospitality" is mentioned.

Hospitality is fundamental to our faith, and your greeters' team could study the biblical accounts that are cited throughout this book. Such study deepens their sense of being part of a team and prepares them to gently educate the congregation. Above all, it equips them to serve with excellence!

Team leader, you can now assess your readiness by reviewing these four questions. If you can answer them categorically and with ease, then set your launch date.

■ Is my team trained?

■ Is my team balanced?

■ Is my team confident?

■ Is my team strategically stratified, not just in a place but in the best spaces needed to be welcoming to each and every worshiper entering the church?

If you can answer yes to each of these questions, then welcome to the ministry of greeting!

ENDNOTES

Chapter 1, The Role of the Greeter
1. David Ben-Gurion, *The Jews in Their Land* (Garden City, NY: Doubleday, 1966), 78.
2. Richard N. Longenecker, *Into God's Presence Prayer in the New Testament* (Grand Rapids: Eerdmans, 2001), 247.
3. Saddleback Church Greeter Ministry Handbook (Saddleback Community Church, Lake Forest, California 2004), 3.

Chapter 2, The Character of the Greeter
1. http://cte.jhu.edu/techacademy/web/2000/kochan/character-traits.html (accessed April 2, 2009).
2. Frederick C. Harrison, *The Spirit of Leadership* (Columbia, TN: Leadership and Development, Inc., 1989), 67.
3. Paige Lanier Chargois, *Certain Women Called by Christ (Biblical Realities for Today)* (Birmingham: New Hope Publishers, 2008).
4. Ibid.
5. Ibid., 239.

Chapter 3, The Character of Your Church
1. Phillip Douglass, *What Is Your Church's Personality?* (Phillipsburg, NJ: P&R, 2008). http://douglassandassociates.com/CPblog/index.php, accessed May 12, 2009.

2. Jim Loehr and Tony Schwartz, *The Power of Full Engagement* (New York: Free Press, 2004), 4.

3. Ibid., 5.

4. Ibid.

5. Ibid.

6. Gilbert Bilezikian, *Community 101* (Grand Rapids: Zondervan, 1997), 43.

7. Ibid., 44.

Chapter 8, Spiritual Development of the Greeter

1. William J. Carter, *Team Spirituality* (Nashville: Abingdon, 1997), 158.

2. Hawaii Geographic Alliance, Copyright © September 1997, updated March 1998, http://www.hawaii.edu/hga/GAW97/greeting.html, accessed March 10, 2009.

3. http://enr.ecnext.com/coms2/article_opedar030616a (accessed April 13, 2009)

4. Emma J. Justes, *Hearing Beyond the Words* (Nashville: Abingdon, 2006), xii.

5. Ibid., xiii.

6. Ibid., 4.

7. Richard N. Longenecker, *Into God's Presence: Prayer in the New Testament* (Grand Rapids: Eerdmans, 2001), 127.

8. Wayne Barber, Eddie Rasnake, and Richard Shepherd, *Life Principles for Worship from the Tabernacle* (Chattanooga, TN: AMG Publishers, 2002), 124.

9. Ibid., 126.

Church Supplies to Aid Your Ministry

Welcome to Our Church

Available in both English and Spanish, this attractively-designed visitor card is a convenient way to welcome visitors and to invite them to join the church. Also provides a means for communicating with members. Size: 2.75" x 4.5". Sold in multiples of 100.
English   55-0003, $8.00
Spanish   Bienvenido/a a nuestra iglesia, SP0553, $8.00

Church Roll and Record Book

Alphabetically record the names of members, church officials, and auxiliary presidents. Also includes ample space to record weddings, baby dedications, funerals, and annual summaries of membership, plus offers 160 additional pages for minutes. Handsomely gold-stamped on red buckram.   55-0272, $22.00 each

What Saith the Scripture?

This booklet for new members contains certificates of baptism and membership, church covenant, and prayer for believers. 32 pages. Gift envelope included. Sold by the dozen.   51-0004, $18.00

The New Member's Guide, Revised   Gordon H. Schroeder

This booklet for new members offers a practical guide to church practices, Bible reading, and prayer as well as an outline of basic Baptist beliefs, a church membership card, and more.
978-0-8170-1436-0, $4.00

To order, call 800-458-3766 or visit www.judsonpress.com.

JUDSON PRESS
PUBLISHERS SINCE 1824

About the Author: Paige Lanier Chargois, MDiv, DMin, is a church consultant in Richmond, Virginia, where she is a member of Saint Paul's Baptist Church. A dynamic and powerful speaker and teacher, Dr. Chargois has served on the staff of several churches, as adjunct faculty and chaplain for universities, and as a leader in nonprofit ministry. As national associate director for Hope in the Cities, she helped to develop processes, training modules, teams, workshops, and conferences that utilized the communicative tool of "honest conversations" or dialogue. She is the author of *Certain Women Called by Christ: Biblical Realities for Today* (New Hope Publishers, 2008).

Book Title: _____

Where did you hear about this book: _____

Reasons why you bought this book: (check all that apply)

☐ Recommendation ☐ Gift ☐ Course/Workshop ☐ Subject ☐ Author ☐ Attractive Cover ☐ Other

We value your feedback. Please provide a review of this book at www.judsonpress.com!

Please send me a Judson Press catalog. I am particularly interested in: (check all that apply)

☐ African American resources ☐ Baptist History/Beliefs ☐ Small Group resources ☐ Other

☐ Christian Education ☐ Church Supplies ☐ Devotional/Prayer _____

Yes, add my name to your mailing list!

Name (print) _____

Street _____

City _____ State _____ Zip _____ Email _____

☐ Please add me to your email promotion list so I can receive special offers and discounts.

☐ I'd like to learn more about the mission of National Ministries, American Baptist Churches USA. Please send information by _____ USPS or _____ e-mail.

Please send a Judson Press catalog to my friend:

Name (print) _____ phone _____

Street _____

City _____ State _____ Zip _____

JUDSON PRESS ▪ PO Box 851 ▪ Valley Forge PA 19482-0851 ▪ **1-800-458-3766** ▪ Fax **(610) 768-2107**

Visit our website at www.judsonpress.com

BUSINESS REPLY MAIL

FIRST-CLASS MAIL   PERMIT NO. 6   VALLEY FORGE PA

POSTAGE WILL BE PAID BY ADDRESSEE

JUDSON PRESS
PO BOX 851
VALLEY FORGE PA 19482-9897